Navajo Rugs

Navajo Rugs

How to Find, Evaluate, Buy, and Care for Them

by DON DEDERA

Foreword by DAN GARLAND

NORTHLAND PUBLISHING

To Cherie Lee, a weaver at heart.

The text type was set in Transitional
The display type was set in Matrix
Composed in the United States of America
Designed by Mary C. Wages
Edited by Stephanie Bucholz
Production supervised by Lisa Brownfield

Manufactured in Hong Kong by ColorCorp, Inc.

Photographs by Don Dedera unless otherwise indicated as follows.
Jerry Jacka: cover, 16, 28, 29 (both), 47, 54, 58 (top), 60, 61, 62, 65 (both), 69,
70, 73, 75, 76, 77 (both), 80 (both), 82 (both), 83, 84, 85, 86, 93, 96, 112
Herb and Dorothy McLaughlin: xii, 3, 8, 63 (both), 66, 71, 74
Gil Mull: 26, 30, 31, 34, 40, 41 (both), 87
Peter Bloomer: 102

Loom illustration on page 21 reprinted from *Working With the Wool:
How to Weave a Navajo Rug,* by Noël Bennett and Tiana Bighorse, © 1971.

COVER: An array of superior Navajo weaves from the inventory of Garland's Navajo Rugs,
Sedona, Arizona. Top to bottom: Serape Revival by Lorelena Begay, 68 x 104 inches;
Teec Nos Pos by Irene Hollie, 50 x 88 inches; Ganado Red by Betty Ann Nez,
61 x 85 inches; Burntwater by Mae S. Nez, 50 x 70 inches. Cover photograph © 1996 by Jerry Jacka
FRONTISPIECE: A rare, woman's wearing blanket, circa 1870–75, combines white warp, and
weft of natural dark and combed gray, indigo, vegetal yellow, and a red, possibly cochineal.
42 x 79 inches. Courtesy San Diego Museum of Man

Rug dimensions refer to weft by warp (see page 14 for definitions of weft and warp).

THIRD EDITION, 1996
Second Printing, November 1997
ISBN 0-87358-635-2

Library of Congress Catalog Card Number 96-10365
Library of Congress Cataloging-in-Publication Data
Dedera, Don.
     Navajo rugs : how to find, evaluate, buy, and care for them / by Don Dedera ;
    foreword by Dan Garland. — 2nd rev. ed.
       p.   cm.
    Includes bibliographical references and index.
    ISBN 0-87358-635-2
     1. Navajo textile fabrics—Collectors and collecting. 2. Rugs—
United States—Collectors and collecting. I. Title.
E99.N3D34   1996
746.7'2—dc20   96-10365

0689/3.5M/11-97

Contents

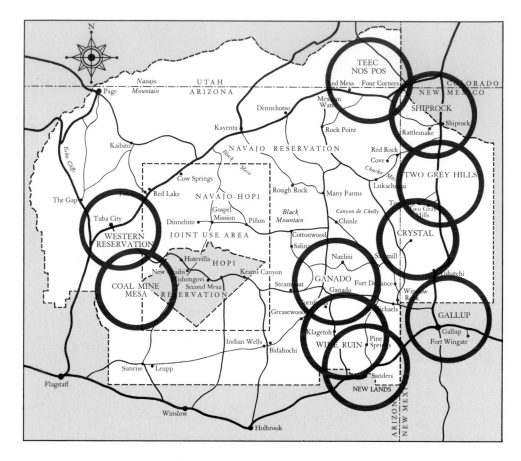

In this map of the Navajo Reservation the names of regional styles (circled) are displayed in the general areas in which they originated. In previous years the areas bearing the type names were the exclusive sources for rugs with the design, colors, etc., associated with those names. Today, however, rugs of all styles are woven throughout the reservation; there are no longer regional rugs, only regional styles.

Foreword

I WAS PICKING APPLES in our Oak Creek Canyon orchard one fall day twenty years ago, when my father came up with the idea that would change my life. He said, "How would you like to start a store with me in Sedona that sells nothing but Navajo rugs?" He talked about the recent boom in Indian Jewelry but also about the rumors he had heard of people using nickel-silver and a threat of imitation jewelry coming from Taiwan. "A Navajo rug cannot be successfully imitated by a machine," he went on. How I was interested. I knew the Navajo and Hopi people came in to trade often in Sedona, but what did I know about Navajo rugs?

Having grandparents who lived their entire lives in Flagstaff, I grew up playing on Navajo rugs that were originally bought in 1910 and still going strong. My first rug was given to me as a college graduation present. It was pulled down from the rafters at the annual Museum of Northern Arizona show. I had hoped to gain information from a friend I had grown up with, but he said all he knew was that "the ones with red are called Ganado Reds." I thought to myself, "So they have names, do they?" The only other name I had heard was Two Grey Hills. I can't tell you how hard I tried to find two mountains in the design.

The next week after my father and I had a talk, he plopped down a stack of books, including Don Dedera's first edition of this book. He said for me to read these and then we would take a trip through the Navajo Reservation. Having graduated from school a year earlier, I was not too eager to burn the midnight oil reading books. But I was quickly drawn into the world of the Navajo people. The history of "the People," or *Diné*, and their trading of goods and ideas with their Pueblo neighbors, the early

Spanish, and later the Americans, gave me a better understanding of contemporary Navajo weaving. After our first trip through the beautiful reservation, braving mountain passes and sliding our way through muddy roads to visit remote trading posts, I was hooked.

Trips to the reservation are fewer now than I would like. The Navajo weavers visit our store daily. I'm always struck by their pride, dignity, and perhaps most of all by their patience. I think it's the face that always stays with you. A noble, proud Diné—or Navajo—face. The weaver is adorned in traditional garb. If it's winter, this means a colorful kerchief around her head, a Pendleton blanket around her shoulders, and a velveteen dress, with the mandatory jewelry giving the finishing regal touch. In her arms she lovingly carries a tightly rolled bundle, wrapped in a sheet or pillow case with safety pins at each end. Inside lies a treasure representing months of her time.

This is the vision one can still see today at trading posts and galleries on or near the Navajo Reservation. I hope it's a vision that never fades. Navajo weaving is flourishing today and a bright future can be forecast.

Certainly the People slowly change. Many now speak English as well as their native tongue. The younger weavers may dress and wear their hair differently from the older weavers, but this is nothing new. The weavings, the beautiful fine masterpieces coming off the looms today, still reflect an inner vision of beauty and balance coupled with a desire to keep tradition alive.

Don Dedera, in his first edition of *Navajo Rugs: How to Find, Evaluate, Buy, and Care for Them,* opened up to the world the vision of these proud, traditional people. Now in its third edition, he again captures the spirit and beauty of this ancient craft kept alive by the Diné. He offers the most up-to-date changes in pattern trends, which typify the Navajo's creativity and ability to adapt to current market demands. In my opinion the uniqueness of this book is its ability to help the newcomer feel comfortable in purchasing their first rug as well as depicting a complete pictorial text for the experienced collector.

I hope that after reading this book you come to the Southwest and experience the land and the tradition of the Diné personally.

Hopefully you will catch the vision I love—of the regal and proud weaver ready to present her weaving for sale. I think nothing demonstrated to me more vividly the pride they have in their craft as a comment my father, Bill Garland, made to me. Many years ago he pointed out, after we had completed a mutually agreeable purchase of a Navajo rug from a weaver, that before leaving she would always take one long, last look at her weaving, which had been such an important part of her life for the last few months.

— Dan Garland
Garland's Navajo Rugs
Sedona, Arizona

I

The Lords of the Earth

THE NAVAJO. *Táá Diné. The People,* they call themselves.

Self-esteem among societies is not uncommon, yet few of the world's cultures cling so tenaciously as Navajo Indians to the notion that they are a superlative people. Even to objective outsiders this Navajo attitude seems justified. Through long, dismal decades they never lost their pride. Through revolutionary changes in geography, in climate, in economy, in politics, they prevailed as a people, retaining essential Navajo traits.

Today they occupy longtime homelands, called *Denétah*. They keep alive their own tongue, practice a religion based on harmony with nature, honor prehistoric family and clan customs, and exalt beautiful objects of individual creation. And in the latter category, tribal ego is expressed most sensationally in the color, design, and refinement of Navajo weaving.

To understand how Diné persevered as a people, it is helpful to know something of the Navajo past. By physique and language they are related to Asia, by kinship with Athapaskan tribes of western Canada and interior Alaska. By legend, the first Navajos emerged from the underground. Anthropologists believe that as nomadic hunters and gatherers they drifted by small bands from A.D. 1100 to 1500 to settle in that part of the American Southwest now known as Four Corners—where New Mexico, Colorado, Utah, and Arizona join.

Here, in the arid, elemental expanses of the high Colorado Plateau country, Navajo capacities for adaptation were supremely tested. To survive in the land of little water they became farmers, borrowing the techniques of Pueblo neighbors. They took up weaving and sandpainting. They adopted (again, according to anthropologists) Puebloan religion and social structure.

When Spaniards began penetrating the Southwest, Indian villages fell one by one and, except during relatively brief revolts, came under foreign rule. Not so the Navajo. Diné faded back into their canyonlands. Along the perimeters of New Spain the Navajos again turned their lives around. They obtained domestic livestock from Spanish herds. Then, devoting less time to farming, they followed flocks of sheep across their vast tablelands. They melded their values with a marvelous, huge animal that was cheaply kept, easily trained, and proudly ridden as fast as the wind.

Navajos afoot were formidable enough, but mounted on swift horses they became, in a grudging Spanish compliment, "The lords of the earth." Neither Spain, Mexico, nor the United States during its first seventeen years of sovereignty in the Southwest succeeded in defeating or dominating the Navajo people.

Their subjugation was brought about by a military strategy now called "scorched earth." In 1863 Colonel Kit Carson swept through Navajoland killing sheep and horses, destroying field crops and homes, and felling whole orchards of peach trees. Only then, at the brink of starvation, did Navajos in substantial numbers submit. In March of 1864, approximately half the tribe—some 8,000 men, women, and children—trudged The Long Walk, 350 miles to Fort Sumner, New Mexico, where officials again thought to convert them to agriculture.

The experiment failed. The soil of the concentration camp was salty. Crops withered. Livestock sickened. Comanche, Mexican, and Anglo bandits preyed upon the Navajo. Over a period of four years, 2,000 Diné died. When costs of feeding the Indians grew prohibitive, Lietenant General William T. Sherman (he of the Civil War march to the sea through Georgia) arrived to make treaty. Navajo leader Barboncito, ill, hungry, impoverished, eloquently pleaded for his people:

> *I hope to God you will not ask me to go to any country except my own . . . I would like to go back the same road we came. . . . After we get back to our country it will brighten up again and the Navajo will be as happy as the land, black clouds will rise and there will be plenty of rain, corn will grow in abundance and everything look happy.*

The return of the Navajo was allowed—to the ashes of burned homes,

to the bones of butchered stock, to the skeletons of girdled fruit trees. For the 12,000 surviving tribespeople, it was the blackest hour in Navajo history. Their recovery in the next sixty years is largely an unsung saga. Beginning in 1869 with an issue of government sheep, the Navajos managed to restore their livestock industry and to increase their own population to 35,000 self-sufficient citizens by 1930.

And again hard times shadowed the Navajo nation. Multiplying herds overgrazed the land, dictating a drastic stock reduction. Overnight, prosperous Navajo families were impoverished. Not until World War II, and its exaggerated demand for manpower, did the Navajo fortunes improve. During the war, 3,600 Navajos served in armed forces, and 15,000 more labored in defense plants. Meanwhile, conditions on the reservation changed little. While postwar America boomed, the Navajo endured chronic problems: tuberculosis, land depletion, poverty, malnutrition. In 1948 there were fewer than 600 full-time jobs for 60,000 Navajos.

A weaver works on a re-creation of an original nineteenth-century rug at Hubbell Trading Post.

Hospital beds numbered 460. On a reservation of sixteen million acres (the size of West Virginia) were exactly 95 miles of paved road. Of 20,000 school-age children, only 6,000 were enrolled.

Today, not "everything look[s] happy," but the *Navajo Times* has boasted, "Better living conditions now prevail throughout the reservation. The People have schools and hospitals. Paved roads now crisscross the land. A 15 dollar sawmill and other industries furnish employment for many Navajos. Tribal parks, civic centers and other recreational facilities provide pleasure for thousands of visitors. Through valuable oil, uranium, coal, helium and other resources, including the education of their young men and women, the tribe has the means to progress to even greater heights."

Modern Navajoland, as the larger nation of which it is a part, exhibits endless contradiction. Every generality is vulnerable. Shining success accompanies mirrored frustration. The aged hermit who has never seen a train is not typical; neither are college graduates administering a multimillion-dollar tribal budget. Longtime sympathizers with the Navajo people learn to accept them as individuals, and to acquire a personal, if fragmented, almanac of impressions.

They number more than 200,000 today, or fifteen times the population at repatriation. Far from vanishing, they are increasing by 3.5 percent annually, at thrice the national birth rate.

Once a many-voiced alliance of extended families, the Navajo nation now governs itself through a tribal chairman elected at large, and by regional representatives to a council. Discovery of petroleum in the 1920s led to the formation of the first Navajo central government.

Fifty thousand Navajos are younger than sixteen years of age. Twenty-five thousand go to school.

At an electronics plant near Fort Defiance, Indians produce hardware that assisted in placing men on the moon. Nearby dwell elders who steadfastly believe their ancestors created the sun by setting afire a huge turquoise stone.

"Literacy" in Navajoland requires fine definition. Only half of the people speak and write English, but 97 percent are fluent in a native language so complex that Navajo radiomen in the Pacific during World War II openly transmitted military secrets and battle orders, a code that was never broken by the Japanese.

Although new homes are rising in settlements throughout the reservation, most Navajo dwellings are without running water. The hogan, a circular, domed, single-room structure of earth-capped logs, poles, or stone is still commonplace. Fried bread, "the pancake of the poor," stretches a diet of mutton and goat, cultivated and wild vegetables, fruits and nuts. Once dominated by staples and sweets from the trading post, in general the Navajo diet is improving with the establishment of modern supermarkets in population centers.

Into the mid-1970s nearly six Navajo families in ten were living on incomes below the poverty line designated by the federal government. The average number of rooms for a Navajo household was two. The average number of people in a Navajo household: five. In more recent years the infant mortality rate, once shamefully high, has been reduced. Life span is increasing. Paved roads total 3,000 miles. Unemployment and underemployment among able-bodied Navajos remains a chronic problem.

Despite a sad past and imperfect present, Navajos tend to be hospitable toward outsiders. Official tribal policy welcomes visitors to camp, fish, and enjoy such spectacles as Canyon de Chelly and Monument Valley. A great-grandson of Barboncito drives a Navajo six-day tour bus. He guides paleface tourists to azure lakes stocked with Navajo trout but he will not eat fish, into which Diné were transformed during the Great Flood. If skeptics ask how Navajos became human again, Barboncito's great-grandson asks for the name of Cain's wife.

Medicine men and women are lawfully recognized as healers in the states where they practice, and rightly so. The recitation of just one ceremony, "The Mountain Way," treatment for epilepsy, requires the equivalent of memorizing exactly the *Episcopal Book of Common Prayer*. The rite lasts nine days, with five hundred songs of twelve verses each. Of about thirty such ceremonies, one healer can master no more than six or eight in a lifetime.

It used to be that every summer some 45,000 Navajos left the reservation in search of work. Many were migrant farm laborers who hoed sugar beets and cultivated truck crops and harvested broom corn, peanuts, cucumbers, and potatoes. But this practice is fading.

In acquiring such a personal almanac, inevitably a friend of the Navajo people will experience an episode similar to this: Into the Tribal Arts and Crafts Center at Window Rock a weaver brings her newest masterpiece of weaving, a three-by-five-foot rug. She receives a wholesale price of $3,000 for her work. Tourists gasp.

They do not realize that for her $3,000 the weaver raised her sheep, sheared them, washed and carded the wool, spun the yarn, and spent every available minute of eighteen months in weaving a fabric that in many respects symbolizes the soul of the undaunted Diné.

2

How Navajo Women
Learned to Weave

SPELLBINDING STORYTELLERS, the Navajo. According to legend:

> Spider Woman instructed the Navajo women how to weave on a
> loom which Spider Man told them how to make. The crosspoles were
> made of sky and earth cords, the warp sticks of sun rays, the healds of
> rock crystal and sheet lightning. The batten was a sun halo, white shell
> made the comb. There were four spindles: one a stick of zigzag light-
> ning with a whorl of cannel coal; one a stick of flash lightning with a
> whorl of turquoise; a third had a stick of sheet lightning with a whorl
> of abalone; a rain streamer formed the stick of the fourth, and its whorl
> was white shell.

Not so romantic is the opinion of the pioneering scholar of Navajo
textiles, Charles Avery Amsden. In a 1935 magazine article he wrote:

> Navajo weaving began, if we really want to go down to the roots,
> long before the Navajo tribe was known in its present location, or had
> ever learned anything about loom weaving. The Pueblo people, who
> were the remote ancestors of those living today, first practiced this great
> craft in the Southwest, using cotton instead of the wool of later times.
> Where they [the Puebloans] learned to cultivate cotton, and spin
> and weave it, is more than we can say, but it is perfectly plain to
> archaeologists who find cotton blankets buried with their dead that
> they were at it at least a thousand years ago and have kept at it down
> to this day. No trace of the Navajo can be found in those early times,

*With her vertical loom
holding weft cords under
strong tension, a Navajo
woman nears the comple-
tion of a twill pattern
double saddle blanket.*

none in fact until almost the time of the Spanish discovery and conquest of the Southwest.

As revealed by archaeology, prehistoric basketmakers artfully wove sandals, bags, nets, and robes of refined plant fibers, furs, and feathers. Weaving of artistic designs and textures flowered among Pueblo III peoples, A.D. 1050–1300. Their descendants continued to weave on unique vertical looms during the centuries that the Navajos were infiltrating Puebloan territory from the north.

Apparently the first generations of Navajos in the Southwest were unschooled in spinning and weaving textiles. Modern Navajos dispute this theory, but the burden of scientific evidence suggests that those early nomads had little patience for cotton-growing or cloth-weaving.

It was Spain that introduced the catalyst—the sheep—which would alter forever the course of Southwestern weaving and Navajo lifeways. Following a long-standing policy of making colonies self-sufficient and profitable, the Spaniards brought sheep by the thousands from Mexico, and decreed that their subjects should weave with wool. Submissive Puebloans obliged.

Concurrently, the Navajos, instinctive hunters and gatherers, acquired some sheep and found them good to eat. By raid and barter they added to their flocks to such an extent that by the mid-1500s Diné were largely a pastoral people, augmenting their mutton diet by trade and casual agriculture. Whether they wove in such early times is conjectural.

Social upheaval and cultural exchange preoccupied Southwestern peoples during the late 1600s. For once, the Pueblos turned on their Spanish masters and drove them back into Mexico. Navajos joined in the rebellion, and afterward, Pueblo people in fear of reprisal took refuge among their Navajo allies. Such fraternizing accelerated when the Spaniards returned with a vengeance in 1692. During these decades of coexistence and intermarriage it is assumed that Navajos learned to weave with wool.

Much mystery has been made of the transfer of weaving talent from one sex to another. Pueblo weavers were, and are, men. Navajo weavers were, and are, women. The explanation is logical enough to Martin Link, former curator of the Navajo Tribal Museum in Window Rock:

This all-wool, handspun, Pueblo-style blanket was collected by J. W. Powell during the 1871–72 exploration of the Colorado River. Natural white, indigo blue, natural black, several patches. 70 x 51 inches. COURTESY THE SAN DIEGO MUSEUM OF MAN

Pueblo men were the cultivators of cotton, and it seemed proper that they should utilize the product of their labor.

When Navajos obtained sheep the men probably considered it beneath their dignity to sit around all day and take care of a flock of tame animals. So the sheep were given to the women and children for care. Gradually the women came to own the sheep. It followed that if women owned the animals, they owned the wool. So to a great extent the women became Navajo weavers.

This first phase chief blanket, circa 1840–50, is made of all-native handspun with brown, white, and blue interrupted stripes, border-to-border, 48 1/2 x 82 inches.
COURTESY THE SOUTHWEST MUSEUM, LOS ANGELES, CALIFORNIA

Whether Navajos were weaving prior to 1700, the craft was well enough along to deserve mention in a 1706 report of the governor of New Mexico. Sketchy references to Navajo weavings are found in Spanish documents through the 1700s. By 1795 Governor Fernando de Chacon wrote of the Navajo, "They have increased their horse herds considerably, they sow much and on good fields; they work their wool with more delicacy and

12

In a conservative example of a second phase chief blanket, circa 1870–80, bayeta bars intrude border-to-border indigo and natural white bands. 46 x 56 inches. COURTESY THE MUSEUM OF NORTHERN ARIZONA

This third phase chief blanket with terraced diamond and symmetrical angles intruding stripes, circa 1860–70, is made of handspun natural white and brown, indigo-dyed handspun, and three-ply rose commercial Saxony yarn. 51 x 69 inches. COURTESY THE SAN DIEGO MUSEUM OF MAN

taste than the Spaniards." Production of Navajo fabrics soared, and trade of blankets and garments dominated Navajo economy. By 1812 a Spanish writer in New Mexico admitted, "Navajo woolen fabrics are the most valuable in our province, and Sonora and Chihuahua as well."

While gaining in popularity abroad, Navajo weaving remained essentially non-European. The spinning was done by hand on a shaft-and-whorl spindle. The foundation yarn (warp) was strung on an upright loom manipulated by simple wooden rods. The woven yarn (weft) was tamped down with a flat batten board. Fabric edges were dressed with extra, twisted yarns. In later times two important Spanish importations were metal shears for fleecing, and metal carders for combing the wool prior to spinning.

Alas, for many a Navajo, their mastery of weaving resulted in enslavement. Through the mid-1800s goodly numbers of Navajo women were captured and impressed into service in the private homes and fabric factories of newly independent Mexico.

Says Martin Link of those dark days, "The slaves were made to weave what their captors dictated, and out of this period emerged a type called the 'slave blanket,' decidedly Mexican in style. Although examples are rare today, their production must have been enormous, because government records speak of 'bales upon bales' of such fabric being carted off to Chihuahua and points south."

Most authorities today regard fragments from Massacre Cave in Canyon del Muerto, northeastern Arizona, to be the most accurately dated pieces of old Navajo weaving. The relic of an 1804–1805 slaughter of Navajos by Spanish soldiers, one remnant (opposite) bears traits of technique and design thought to be of Navajo origin.

Displayed at the Museum of Northern Arizona in Flagstaff is a fragment of a patchwork shoulder blanket, found by Leland C. Wyman in Canyon de Chelly in 1933. Upon an original blanket of brown wool with white stripes were sewn a grab-bag of fabrics—one scrap as coarse as burlap, a corner of a Hopi woman's dress, and possibly a swatch of fine, imported Spanish cloth. On the basis of design and dyes, curators believe some of the fragments may predate Massacre Cave.

"Despite the fact that there are as yet no earlier examples of Navajo textiles," writes Clara Lee Tanner, "the Massacre Cave pieces indicate a tradition of long standing in materials and decoration. . . . The consensus

Among the earliest dated Navajo weaves, this dress fragment was recovered from Canyon del Muerto's Massacre Cave, where Spaniards had slain a number of Indians in 1804–1805. The Museum of Northern Arizona has a patchwork cloak found in Canyon de Chelly by Leland C. Wyman in 1933 which may, on the basis of design and dye, contain fragments of weaving that predate this Massacre Cave remnant. Approximately 36 x 36 inches. COURTESY THE MUSEUM OF NORTHERN ARIZONA

is that plain tapestry weave, natural wool colors, a little native dye, indigo, and bayeta, and simple striped patterns predominated until the middle of the nineteenth century."

In the following century, as exemplified by their weaving, the genius of the Navajo people for adaptation would be supremely tempted and tested.

3

From Dingy Sheep
to Exquisite Rug

JUST AS THE NAVAJO PEOPLE DEFEAT GENERALITY, so does their weaving. For every rule regarding Navajo rugs, there are rule-breakers. That said, construction of Navajo fabric has remained remarkably constant. For some three hundred years, there have occurred no marked changes in weaving, especially in the preliminary stages.

Excellent, definitive studies of Navajo weaving are available. One, *Working with the Wool*, by Noël Bennett and Tiana Bighorse, explains precisely, step by step, how a Navajo rug can be woven—even by non-Indians. Other books analyze techniques of individual weavers, past and present. But for this introduction, risking exceptions, generally a Navajo rug passes through the following phases from fleece to floor.

GROWING THE WOOL

Less so than in the past, stockraising continues as an important Navajo industry. The imported Spanish peasant breed that constituted original Navajo flocks were scrawny of flesh but long and straight of wool. Such fleeces tended to tangle and attract debris in the arid, thorny Southwestern pastures; but once clean, *churro* wool was ideal for spinning. During the late 1800s the American government issued strains of Spanish Merino and French Rambouillet. The common Navajo type of this day yields better mutton but shorter, kinkier wool, not the easiest raw material for weaving. These sheep produce shorter fibers but about twice as much wool by weight. As of old, the herding is left to women and girls who, by custom, come into ownership of individual sheep.

Under the shadows of Skeleton Mesa, a band of Navajo sheep and goats dine on hay in a traditional deadwood corral. The sheep are freshly shorn before their scheduled return to the open range.

Usually in May or June the sheep are sheared when the fleece is thickest. In early times the wool was cut with a knife or sharpened metal scrap; now it is done with simple shears resembling lawn clippers. Snipping from neck to tail, the shearer tries to keep the fleece intact. Best wool for weaving is from the back, shoulders, and flanks. Fiber deemed too short for hand-spinning is sold by the bag to traders and to tribal cooperatives for resale as far away as Japan.

CLEANING

Vigorous shaking is sometimes all that's required to remove grit and twigs. Burrs must be removed by hand. A native soap, of yucca root extract, chases dirt without driving out the lanolin which gives a Navajo rug its long life. The wool is fluffed and dried in the hot sun, said to make it stretch better in spinning. To whiten wool some weavers sprinkle it with kaolin or gypsum.

CARDING

Cards made commercially are thin boards armed with myriad wire teeth and fastened with handles. A wad of tangled wool is placed on one card, then repeatedly combed between the two until fibers lie in the same direction.

Before an octagonal hogan, which once served as a guest house for Hubbell Trading Post, Elizabeth Kirk combs white wool with metal-toothed carders.

A ballet of the hands accompanies the spinning of carded wool upon a wooden spindle. Inertia is imparted to the flywheel by working the spindle against the thigh.

At this step natural gray wool is obtained by carding light and dark wool together. The wool comes off the cards in a fluffy roll. Hand carding adds to the uniformity and strength of Navajo yarns. Carding further cleans the wool, but it's the weaver's hardest chore, so today many weavers buy pre-carded wool from commercial suppliers.

SPINNING

The spinning wheel is unknown to the Navajo. In its place is a relic inherited from those days when Navajos traveled light. The spindle is a stick about twenty inches long. Near one end of the stick is a wooden disk, which acts as a flywheel when the right hand rubs the spindle against the right thigh. Meantime the left hand feeds carded wool onto the long, pointed end of the spindle. All the while the spinner adjusts the tension on the strand to achieve uniform size. Navajo homespun, with a left-hand twist, is opposite most other Indian homespun and commercial yarns, which are right-handed.

All Navajo yarn is spun at least twice; some three and four times (up to ten times for tapestries), with each spinning improving tightness, smoothness, and fineness. Foundation yarn, called warp, must be respun several times.

DYEING

The Navajo passion for color has been satisfied in complicated ways down through the years. Red flannel by the wagonload was raveled and retwisted in early times and, as discussed in Chapter 4, garish fads invaded Navajo weaving when commercially dyed yarns reached the trading posts. Today weavers may restrict themselves to natural white, brown, and black, or mixtures of these. They may use aniline dyes from the white man's world. Or, as the trend seems to be, they may draw upon a hundred or more natural dyes which utilize the roots, barks, leaves, and fruits of dried plants of their region. Vegetal dyeing of a batch might be repeated daily for as long as a week. Dyes are set with various chemicals, sometimes in earlier days an acid such as urine.

SETTING UP THE LOOM

As depicted in detail in the sketch (opposite), the Navajo vertical loom consists of a sturdy frame within which are suspended, joined, and anchored a series of horizontal wooden bars, each with a vital function. A pair of conveniently spaced trees might serve as frame posts. For winter work the loom might be anchored by stones and buried beneath the earthen hogan floor. Sets of foundation warps are arranged between upper and lower loom bars. One advantage of the vertical loom is constant control over the tension applied to the warps.

Alternating warps are separated by a shed rod. This separation can be reversed by pulling on the heddle, attached by loose loops to alternating sets of warps.

As in most arts, the foundation is crucial to success. In a fine contemporary Navajo rug that is three by five feet, the warps may total 240. This requires 400 yards of handspun yarn—four lengths of a football field. All this, and weaving is yet to begin.

WEAVING

By pushing the shed rod, or pulling on the heddle, alternating sets of warp are moved back and forth. A batten, a swordlike stick of polished and shaped hardwood, further separates these sets of warps, to allow insertion of the horizontal weft threads. Weaving begins at the bottom, the weaver drawing upon a mental image of the complete rug. Weft threads are

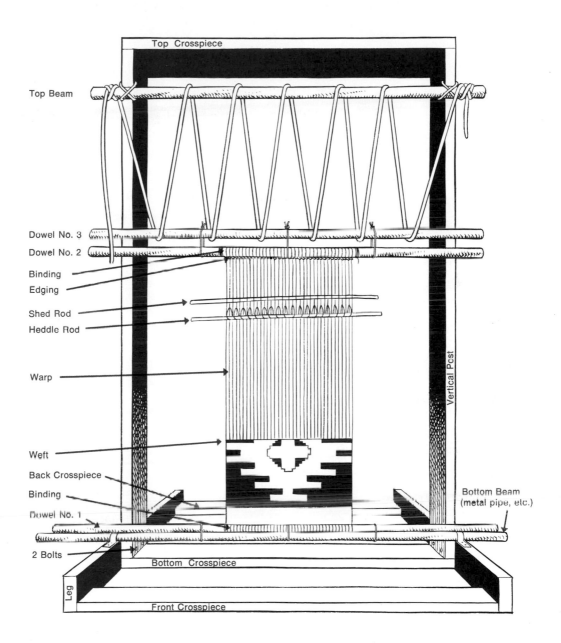

Top Crosspiece

Top Beam

Dowel No. 3

Dowel No. 2

Binding

Edging

Shed Rod

Heddle Rod

Warp

Weft

Back Crosspiece

Binding

Dowel No. 1

2 Bolts

Bottom Crosspiece

Leg

Front Crosspiece

Vertical Post

Bottom Beam
(metal pipe, etc.)

21

pounded down with a wooden comb and a batten. As the warps are moved back and forth they disappear under the wefts, giving the Navajo weave its distinctive tapestry finish. By custom the weaver sits on soft skins of goat or sheep. She weaves off small balls of naturally colored or dyed weft. When the work rises higher than she can reach, she may slacken the tension bar and sew fast the completed section to the lower loom bar, or the loom bars may be adjusted to lower the work level. Again the warp is tightened and the weaving continues. But now her design reference is hidden; she must remember where she went, to know where to go. The last few inches of weft are inserted from the top down. For this, a needle may be used. Along most Navajo weaves are edges reinforced with extra, twisted warps, characteristically of the same yarn that forms the main background design color.

From the kit of a typical Navajo weaver are the hand tools of the craft. Clockwise from top left: Hardwood combs, commercial carding boards, steel shears from England, long, thin battens whittled of juniper wood, and spindle and flywheel for spinning.

SPECIAL WEAVING

Aside from regular tapestry weaving on a standard loom arrangement some Navajo women specialize in other techniques of long-standing tradition. Several variations of twill weaving go into saddle blankets and larger rugs. An array of as many as five heddles lets the weaver choose unequal sets of warps, such as under-three, over-one, to produce textured diamonds, terraces, and zigzags. In such rugs designs of the two faces of fabric are the same, but the colors are opposed.

Mental concentration plus manual dexterity go into the so-called "two-face" rug. Again, with multiple heddles, a few weavers today produce rugs of different colors *and* designs on the two faces. Gaining in acceptance among artists and admirers is the "raised outline" weave, in which color and design are enhanced by an etched effect of raised wefts.

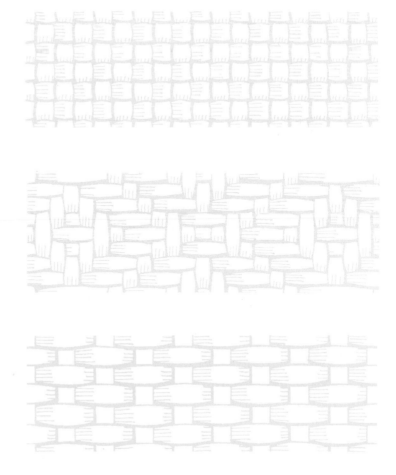

Among the eight distinct Navajo weaves is the plain or basket weave, commonplace and probably the oldest. Warp and weft are equally distinct in the finished fabric.

Borrowed from Puebloan weavers, the diamond twill is also quite common. A relief pattern is created by arranging the heddles to elevate groups of warp.

Another familiar pattern is the tapestry weave. The warp is covered by beating down the weft to compress the threads together. It is a plain but very effective weave.

4

Pueblo Looms, Spanish Sheep, Navajo Artistry

"IT OFTEN HAPPENS," observes Martin Link, long-time publisher of *The Indian Trader*, "that when a culture experiences strife, stress, and chaos, the people turn to their art to express themselves eloquently. Some of the best of literature, painting, and architecture was produced by societies enduring hard times. This is the history of Navajo weaving. While Navajo religion, economy, life-style, and land base were under attack, weaving art reached new peaks of achievement."

The Classic period, experts call it. Although arbitrarily bracketed between the years 1850 and 1870, some authorities believe the tradition of excellence was established as early as 1800. Material examples are scarce, but it is supposed that Navajos were splendid spinners and weavers of tapestry fabrics modestly beautified by border-to-border natural colors.

Indigo dye from Europe arrived in the Southwest in the early 1800s, and some of the rich, deep blue began appearing as end stripes on Navajo blankets. By mid-century vegetal yellows and greens were occasionally used along with natural white, brown, and black wool. Many classic period weaves were of single-strand, handspun wool. Black wool might be darkened with a mixture of sumac, ochre, and piñon pitch. Extract of goldenrod mixed with indigo made green. A sunny yellow was derived from rabbit brush blossoms.

But nothing brightened up Navajo weaving so much as *bayeta* red. A myth persists that early Navajo weavers removed red uniforms from the bodies of slain Spanish soldiers and converted the wool into blankets. In truth, all the armies of Spain couldn't have supplied enough red uniforms for the classic period. And no self-respecting Navajo would touch an item tainted by *ch'įįdii*, the ghost of death.

This classic serape, circa 1870, tightly woven to the texture of canvas, contains natural white handspun, indigo handspun, yellow, green, and red Saxony, and 5 1/2-inch bands of red bayeta near each end. 48 1/2 x 68 inches. COURTESY THE GIL MULL COLLECTION

The story of *bayeta* is romantic enough and undoubtedly far-fetched. In limited amounts it may have reached Navajoland in the form of red flannel underwear, which the Indians had no qualms against pilfering from Spanish clotheslines. Perhaps some weavers unraveled some long johns and threaded the strands into new blanket patterns. At any rate, the Spaniards, detecting a demand, began importing English-made baize, via Spain and Mexico. It arrived by the bolt, as bayeta, a scarlet-to-crimson answer to every red-loving Navajo's prayer. Bayeta's color was imparted by the dye, cochineal, extracted from dry, crushed insects native to Mexico and other warm climates.

Incredibly, Navajo weavers so treasured bayeta they would ravel the cloth strand by strand. Then they would twist together two, three, and sometimes four or more thin plies of bayeta to form multiple weft yarn. Even so, the bulk of classic period fabric was built upon single-ply, fine homespun.

Turkish flannels, English serges, and Mexican yarns, although inferior, competed with bayeta. In fact, much of what is considered bayeta today may be of American trade goods. As American presence grew, wagons groaning with bolts of sleazy Eastern woolens traveled eight hundred miles

This transitional child's serape, circa 1880s, is of Germantown yarns. Such designs are customarily called "Spider Woman" crosses. 34 x 45 inches. COURTESY THE HEARD MUSEUM, PHOENIX, ARIZONA

down the Santa Fe trail toward a tribe of weavers who literally could make something out of nothing.

The ingenuity of classic weaving is demonstrated in a child's shawl, thirty by fifty-five inches, now in the collection of Charles G. (Gil) Mull. The warp consists of five distinctly different types of yarn: brown handspun, soft maroon, and white Saxony, a tightly twisted yellow three-ply yarn, and a very tightly twisted white three-ply yarn. Some warps were paired, others were single strands.

No less than eleven different wool materials form the weft, handspun, raveled, and commercial. Speculates Mull, "The extreme diversity of yarns in this blanket suggests that the weaver was scraping the bottom of the barrel for every bit of available material. The almost total absence of white handspun wool, even in the warp, suggests a scarcity. It is tempting to

In wearing positions are hung (left) a classic second phase chief blanket, circa 1865, and (right) a late third phase chief blanket, circa 1875. COURTESY THE HEARD MUSEUM

wonder if this blanket could have been woven during the time of the Navajo captivity at Bosque Redondo (1864–68). During this period the Navajo were largely cut off from their normal supplies of wool, and machine-spun Saxony yarns are reported to have been supplied from the Fort Sumner post supplies. . . ."

At any rate, toward the latter part of the classic period the Navajos acquired their first commercial yarns. Perhaps at Fort Sumner, deprived of their flocks, weavers began to use Saxony from Germany. Almost pastel of hue and silky soft, three-ply Saxony often was combined with bayeta and natural handspun. Saxony also came in colors other than red.

Stripes remained popular throughout the classic period, but gradually a Mexican-like, stair-stepped diamond intruded Navajo taste. Geometric designs, beginning small, were dropped into the edge-to-edge stripes; the diamonds and zigzags enlarged until the background stripes were all but lost. This progression is most clearly followed in the so-called "chief" blanket.

Navajos had no chiefs. The blanket of that name largely was an export item, prized by the Plains Indians. First cousin to the Pueblo *manta*, the chief blanket was for throwing about the shoulders in foul weather. Thus worn, the stripes complimented the physique of the puniest brave. To more easily form these stripes, Navajo weavers made the warp dimension the shortest so that wefts could be run from edge to edge. Black, white, indigo blue, and bayeta culminated in a final phase of "chief" boasting elaborate crosses, triangles, and diamonds. An estimated 90 percent of "chief" and other wearing blankets were traded to Cheyenne, Kiowa, Sioux, Comanche, and Arapaho Indians rich enough to afford them, and to other men who wanted to appear larger than life.

Less striking garments were also woven, some for Navajo use. Muted designs marked women's wear, usually three bands of repeated designs, running the width of the blanket. Another traditional clothing for women of this time was the *biil,* a dress made of two identical, rectangular blankets.

Softly uniform in weave, this serape, circa 1880–90, presents a riot of natural and aniline-dyed handspun, raveled red flannels, and green commercial yarn. 53 x 80 inches. COURTESY THE GIL MULL COLLECTION

Custom decreed that a broad black center band would be bracketed by bands of red, preferably bayeta. The idea for the biil may have survived a time when Navajo women wore two animal furs sewn together as a poncho with holes for head and arms.

The most astonishing part of the classic period was the bayeta serape, a radical departure in design and color from the calm natural stripes of Pueblo origin. Exactly when and how the idea of terraced diamond motifs arrived in the Southwest is conjectural. The first examples of the Navajo bayeta serape are tentatively dated from 1830–50.

"The *bayeta* serape was an object produced to astound and impress," write Mary Hunt Kahlenberg and Anthony Berlant. "Fine, rare materials influenced the elaborateness of design and inspired weaving of the highest quality. Patterns in the *bayeta* serape literally burst across the blanket. . . . The design often appears as a variation of superimposed diamonds over stripes." Frequently the background is of raveled bayeta woven into horizontal stripes of blue and white.

Of similar serape shape was another exceptional blanket, the classic period *moki*. Hinting of Pueblo genius, the pattern was of black, brown, and blue weft stripes. Parallelograms of white and red in later years were inserted to break up the stripes, but relative to the bayeta serape, the moki (from an old term for the Hopi Pueblo Indians) remained a conservative product of the classic period.

The decline and near collapse of Navajo weaving during the last third of the nineteenth century is ascribed to many factors. At repatriation from Fort Sumner, Navajo flocks numbered fewer than two thousand head. Trading posts came to the reservation in the 1870s, and the railroad in the 1880s. Commercial yarns, dyed in a rainbow of colors and ready to weave, tempted weavers into shortcuts and wild experiments. By 1890 weavers had come under tremendous economic pressures to cater to the preconceptions—however preposterous—that white tourists held of Indian design. One result: if an Indian craft, surely it must be covered with swastikas, arrows, and superstitious signs. It would take the women about twenty years to recover from this Transition Period, which witnessed some of the worst Navajo weaving produced for often tasteless patrons.

5

The Blanket That
Went on the Floor

RAW, IRRESISTIBLE CHANGE was thrust upon the Navajo nation in the years of Fort Sumner and afterward. Majority histories refer to the process as the civilizing of the Wild West.

But in countless ways for Indian people the intrusion of an industrialized society was disastrous, demeaning, and demoralizing. "Improvements," well-intended as they may have been by Americans and their government, in some ways altered Indian life for the better, but as often as not something of value was lost. For the Navajo, one price of Americanization was classic weaving.

Until about 1875 the products of Navajo looms were blankets for their own wear and for trading to other Indians. By the 1880s stores operated by white traders sprang up in the most remote corners of the reservation. The shelves of the trading posts offered clothing, utensils, and processed food. Inexpensive, machine-made blankets from Pendleton, Oregon, appealed to women who heretofore might spend half a year weaving a blanket of similar size. The art of weaving might have perished altogether had it not been for another factor in the trading business—the demand by tourists for Indian curios. Trainloads of white customers were sold native crafts by the ton by large firms such as the Fred Harvey Company. Far away from the railroad, a Navajo weaver might wear a cotton skirt, velvet blouse, and Pendleton blanket, but her handwork would bring cash and credit at her trading post. Some enterprising traders stimulated sales with the mailing of brochures with pictures of available weaves.

From the beginning of this commerce traders influenced what buyers wanted. In time, what buyers wanted, buyers got. They demanded pillow

This serape, entirely of commercial wool yarn in ten colors on a cotton warp, circa 1899–1900, is the essence of Germantown. 52/54 x 74 inches.
COURTESY THE GIL MULL
COLLECTION

faces, lap robes, and bed covers. Some blankets of high quality continued to be made, but the rush was toward inferior, quickly woven items for decorating white homes.

And if homespun was scarce, or required so much time and work, the trader had another answer: commercial yarns—dyed, spun, twisted, and ready to weave. Called "Germantown," after the textile center in Pennsylvania, the full spectrum of aniline-dyed, three- and four-ply yarns was imported. Navajo weavers went on a color binge. It was as if artists limited all their lives to black, red, blue, and white suddenly held palettes daubed with fifty hues. In explosive "eye-dazzlers" and other intense, expressionistic styles, Navajo weavers outdid one another in creating optical effects.

Germantown yarn was expensive; aniline dye was cheap. Sold for the first time in bulk in the 1880s, aniline dyes derived from coal tar were simple to use (just toss the packet into boiling water, sometimes envelope and all), garish, and exactly what white folk wanted in authentic Navajo rugs—lots of bright color. Navajo weavers substituted commercial cotton twine, available for the first time in substantial amounts, for the stronger wool warp spun by hand.

Designs also gave way to new ideas. Instead of the right-angle terraces of the Classic Period, Navajo weaving came to be dominated by the smooth-sided diamond and triangle. This *serrate* or diamond pattern often ran the length of the weave.

Nudged by the businessman in the middle, both weavers and customers by 1890 came to consider a Navajo tapestry a suitable covering for the floor. This transformation of a blanket to a rug affected size, texture, and design. For one thing, rugs seemed more proper with borders.

In a gross departure from their long tradition of abstract design, Navajo weavers obliged public demand with a new kind of rug: the pictorial. They wove American flags, trading post signs, mottos, figures of cows,

The design of this classic eye-dazzler of Germantown yarn, circa 1890, is dominated by a multihued, eight-pointed star. 25 x 39 inches. COURTESY THE SAN DIEGO MUSEUM OF MAN

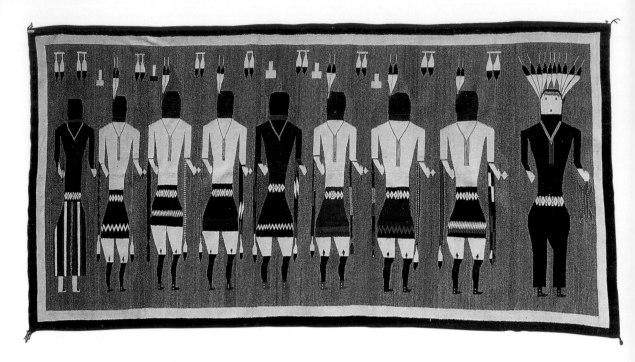

horses, houses, birds, bows and arrows, and cowboys. In 1896, with the completion of the Denver and Rio Grande Railroad in Durango, the high point of the celebration was the presentation of a Navajo blanket depicting a five-car passenger train and a railroad station in each corner. Strongly opposed by fellow tribesmen, weavers just after the turn of the century began to picture *yeis,* Navajo divinities, in their rugs.

The mid-1880s brought a reduction in the use of commercial yarns. Navajo flocks had multiplied, and local wool was abundant. The reservation in general produced weaves of ever-declining quality. A common practice of traders was to purchase rugs by weight, with little regard for the success of design or technique. For these "pound blankets" wholesalers paid from twenty-five cents to two dollars and fifty cents per pound. As human as any other people, the Navajos soon learned that a rug greasy with lanolin and laden with sand would bring more than a clean fabric of careful construction.

Although much maligned in some accounts of Navajo history, traders of this period as best they could probably saved and eventually revitalized Navajo weaving.

Among early champions of quality work were Lorenzo Hubbell of Ganado, and J. B. Moore of Crystal. At Chinle, beginning about 1920,

This yeibichai rug made in 1942 between Oraibi and Indian Wells, Arizona, is of handspun wool warp, and wefts of handspun in natural white, black, and brown, and more handspun in aniline colors. 78 x 142 inches. COURTESY THE SAN DIEGO MUSEUM OF MAN through the efforts of white helpers and Indian experimenters, interest was rekindled in vegetal dyes. Formulas by the score were perfected using ingredients of nature. Although few of the concoctions likely were used in early times, the muted colors are somewhat remindful of some found in antique Southwestern weaving.

In the half century between 1920 and 1970 the clearest direction for Navajo rugs was identification of types by geographic origin. Again, the trader played a role. After World War II rug designs and types became standardized around trading posts such as Two Grey Hills, Wide Ruin, and Teec Nos Pos. By no means were all rugs tied to a reservation region, but the trend was strong, fueled by maturing appreciation of collectors and neighborhood pride of weavers.

As always, economic forces continued to influence Navajo weaving. During the Great Depression a relative few weavers remained at their looms despite miserable rewards. Yet it was during these years that the largest Navajo rug in history was constructed, by the Joe family of Greasewood.

This "pound" blanket of heavy handspun on cotton warp, circa 1880, is evidence of a troubled time. Its design is filled with the cultural conflicts of border-to-border stripes, frets, swastikas, and lozenges. 61 x 64 inches. AUTHOR'S COLLECTION

This well-made wedge-weave blanket, circa the 1880s, is entirely of hand-spun, natural brown, and white, and dyed with indigo, aniline red, and, possibly, vegetal yellow. Also called pulled-warp construction, the weave is characterized by scalloped edges. 62 x 61 inches. COURTESY THE GIL MULL COLLECTION

In a special stone house forty feet long Julia Joe and her two daughters, Lilly and Emma, began processing wool. Beginning in 1932 the women sheared sixty white sheep and eighteen black. Two full years went into carding, spinning, and dyeing. Then, from sunrise to midnight for three years and three weeks the women wove their masterpiece, a seamless rug measuring twenty-six by thirty-six feet and weighing 250 pounds.

For their heroic labor they earned about ten cents an hour. In 1938 a trader kept an accounting of a typical weaver's investment of time, and he concluded that she was making no more than a dollar a day.

According to veteran trader Russell Foutz, Navajo textile art fell into hard times again in the 1950s, when staple wool became scarce. Foutz attributes a revival to the breeding of native ewes with Lincoln rams, noted for longer, kinkier wool:

> *It was only after commercial yarn was made available that many women who had never made a rug before started to weave. A great number of them learned their art by weaving with Germantown, and then graduated to handspun as they became more expert.*
>
> *I am convinced that if it had not been for commercially prepared wool there is no doubt that Navajo weaving would be a lost art today.*

TOP: *This eye-dazzler rug is a rainbow of handspun in natural, indigo, and hues of aniline, plus a center stripe of dark rose bayeta, and has commercial tassels, serrated diamond patterns, and pre-1890 Greek fret borders. 45 x 71 inches.* COURTESY THE GIL MULL COLLECTION

RIGHT: *This late classic serape in typical moki pattern is of natural white and brown-black handspun, indigo handspun, and raveled American flannel, circa 1875. 52 x 72 inches.* COURTESY THE GIL MULL COLLECTION

*As a page from Gil Mull's
original 1911 J. B. Moore
rug catalog attests, Navajo
weaving sold by the square
foot in the early years of
the twentieth century.
Shown on the opposite page
is a matching rug, which
has left Mull's ownership
to take a place in the
Denver Museum of Natural
History.*

PLATE XXV

Special Design and Weave by "Yeh del-spah-bi-Mah."

From "ER-20" class, original 64x85 inches in size. A new pattern that has not been introduced yet, but one which we are confident will prove a "winner." Will be made up as shown and in other colors according to the weaver's fancy, and as the results of their variations show.

"ER-20" class, stock size 43x76 inches up to 6x9 feet. Price, 90c to $1.00 per square foot, or $21.00 to $23.50 for small ones, and up or down for others in proportion. Made to order in any size and colors desired at price proportioned to size.

None in "T-XX" class. Not made to order in this class. Price, $41.00.

In flux as always, Navajo weaving today has broken out of a system that presumed that women of certain areas would weave specific patterns. Contemporary weavers are well traveled and some dwell far from their places of birth. Provincial loyalties are being replaced with a new sense of Navajo *nation*. The women attend fairs and exhibitions where their weaves are shown side by side. Just as a new England dory can be manufactured in San Diego, so may a Teec Nos Pos outline pattern grace a loom at Kayenta.

The happy reality of these times is that Navajo women in goodly numbers have elevated their inheritance once again to an art form. As in the past, the weavers have borrowed and adapted ideas and new designs and varied techniques within their ever-dynamic craft. For once the doomsayers were wrong. In the 1990s the best Navajo weaving compares with the finest of the Classic Period.

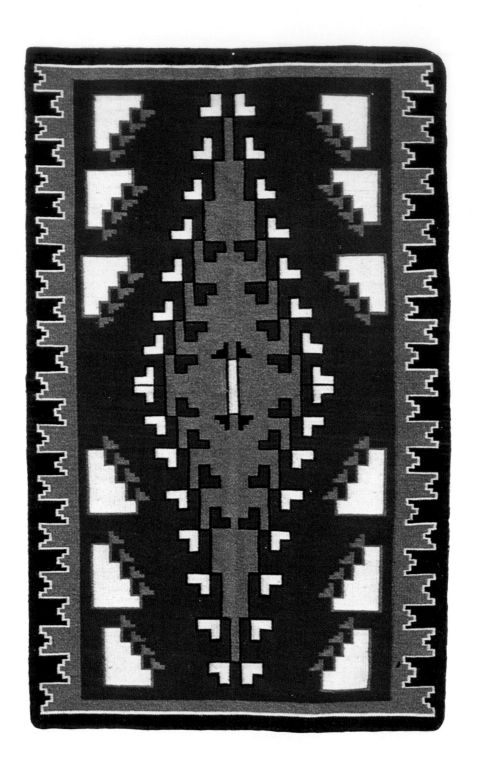

6

Contemporary is Cosmopolitan

ON A TOUR OF HIS OLD HAUNTS, a retired white trader during the 1970s stopped at a trading post near Shiprock, New Mexico. He was surprised to note that not one sandpainting rug—for which the region was famed—could be seen.

"Where are all your ceremonial rugs?" the former trader asked the current trader.

"Don't have any," he replied. "All my weavers are making Two Grey Hills. That's what the public wants!"

For many years two tiny settlements in the far western end of Navajoland were the source of a special kind of weave called "Raised Outline" in which color design is emphasized by a thickening of weft. By the 1970s weavers at Ganado, halfway across the reservation, were producing Raised Outline rugs. By 1980 the fretted, bordered pattern associated with Ganado could come from anywhere. When that selfsame old trader wanted a Tuba City Storm pattern rug for his own collection, he commissioned a weaver at Old Sawmill to do it based on a favorite photograph.

If anything, the blurring of regional origins for regional patterns accelerated through the 1980s and continues through the 1990s.

Although the geographical names no longer guarantee origin, the terms are still meaningful and useful. Weavers, exhibitors, traders, and buyers often continue to categorize by regional name if not by geography. Of course, some weaves, notably saddle blankets, never were limited to a specific locale. Today, as in the past, saddle weaves may originate almost any place.

The elongated central diamond of a typical red Ganado is captured in a modern weaving of handspun native wool, and predyed, commercial "wool-top," also handspun, by Elizabeth and Helen Kirk. 36 x 60 inches. COURTESY HUBBELL TRADING POST, GANADO, ARIZONA

Given the gamut of commercial yarns and dyes, contemporary weavers have access to an infinite variety of color. Much of the raw material continues to be shorn from Navajo animals; the sheep population of the Navajo nation today is stabilized at about two million head. Yet many weavers find the abundance of pre-spun commercial yarn irresistible. Buying manufactured yarn bypasses the onerous tasks of shearing, cleaning, dyeing, carding, and spinning.

As throughout the past, nearly all current production is of simple tapestry weave; that is, weft passes over and under alternating warps. The weft threads are tamped down with a wooden comb and batten, so as to hide the warp. The most popular shape continues to be rectangular, with warps running the length.

Regarding price, better specimens have more than outpaced the inflation of the past three decades. As with rare coins, prized postal stamps, and fine antiques, well-made and maintained Indian arts and crafts have generally appreciated in value, especially Navajo rugs. A gentleman of acquaintance, after thirty-five years of long, hard toil in the printing business, retired with about one-third of a million dollars.

"Instead of all that risk and all that struggle," he said, "I would have done better pumping gasoline at minimum wage, and buying one little Navajo saddle blanket every Friday." Of course, the same could be said of fine shotguns, Scottsdale acreage, and Model A Fords. But it's difficult to name another collectible that has gained more in worth than Navajo weaving over the past half century.

With their compensation improving, weavers are continuing a trend toward smaller pieces, of a size and weight approximating those of the Classic Period shoulder blanket, and toward the modern notion of creating tapestries obviously intended for hanging. More so than ever before, the blanket that went on the floor now goes on the wall.

As for regional types, fads come and go. Demand was high fifteen or twenty years ago for storm patterns. That vogue passed and is now coming back. Widely distributed, high-quality newspaper, magazine, and book photographs have made regional patterns available to all weavers. In 1978 I met a weaver at an arts fair in Albuquerque, New Mexico. She was from Gallup, yet showing a fine rug done in a traditional Ganado, Arizona, pattern.

"Where did you get the idea to do this?" I asked.

She said, "Oh, I took it from your book!"

Change: the unchanging nature of the Navajo culture. In 1963 Indian trader Gilbert Maxwell coined a term, "the general rug." His rough estimate was that rug production was 50 percent saddle blankets, 25 percent general rugs, 25 percent specific and distinctive as to type and region. "The general rug," he wrote, "is the rug whose design, quality, and color do not distinguish it as being from any particular locale. They may be plain stripes or geometric patterns with or without a border. Such rugs are made throughout the reservation."

Regional Rugs

GANADO

If contemporary weaving boasts a capital, it is Ganado, just south of the geographical center of the Navajo nation. No better introduction to the evolution and status of Navajo textiles exists on the reservation than Hubbell Trading Post, just west of Ganado. It is also an ideal place for learning about Navajo ways.

Now a National Historic Site under park service supervision, Hubbell's is the oldest continuously operated trading post on the reservation. It was established in 1876. Existing buildings date to the turn of the century. Indians travel from miles around to shop among the tobacco tins, "can good," horse collars, kerosene lanterns, and bolts of velvet. To Hubbell's they still bring their wool, their rugs, their jewelry, their crops of piñon nuts. For the Navajo people the Hubbell post is a social center, gossip exchange, and political forum. The Navajo tongue freely commingles with tourist talk. Once weavers demonstrated their skills in the adjoining stone-and-sod warehouse. Now women handspin yarn and weave on upright looms in the visitors center. Rugs representative of all sections of the reservation are stacked shoulder-high in the trading post rug room, where for more than a century woven Navajo masterworks have been bought and sold.

Reflexive as it is to malign the white trader among Indians, Don Lorenzo Hubbell's role among the Navajo community was friend, champion, helper. Of a family of New Mexican traders, Hubbell dared to take over a store in a hostile land beyond the protection of the U.S. Army in 1876. He survived and prospered because he was fair, wise, ambitious, and more than a little lucky. Once he was tied to a post for death by torture and was saved only by the unlikely arrival of a Navajo ally.

Don Lorenzo was more than a trader. He brought the best of literature and art to his remote and earthen home. To his table were attracted President Theodore Roosevelt, painters, sculptors, writers, scientists, and philosophers. Hubbell was active in Arizona politics. When the papers of statehood were signed in Washington in 1912, directly behind President Taft stood Don Lorenzo. Hubbell was a main force in bringing the Petrified Forest and Painted Desert under federal protection.

At its crossroads of commerce, the rambling Hubbell hacienda thrived. Hubbell issued his own aluminum money. Indian herders and craftsmen depended upon Hubbell's just heart and fluent Navajo. During economic slumps Hubbell cheered weavers by insisting upon and paying for quality work. Through the 1880s Hubbell resold $25,000 worth of rugs a year to the Fred Harvey Company. At times the blanket room was piled to the ceiling.

"Collecting is a disease," Don Lorenzo's daughter once declared. "In this case, the whole family caught it."

The trading post became an archive of the best in arts and crafts, and today it is virtually as Hubbell left it, hung with rare Southwestern blankets, stocked with firearms, furnished with fixtures of surprising

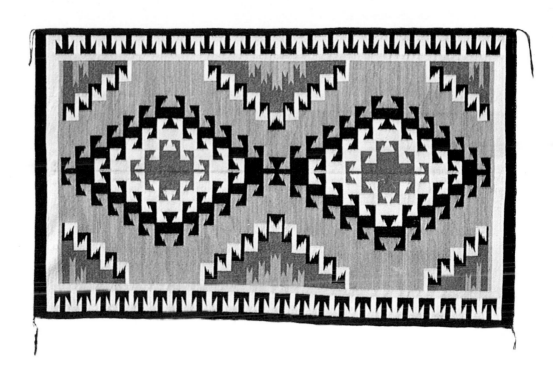

TOP: *This is a one-of-a-kind rug. The style is usually done in Ganado red, but on impulse it was produced in blue by Mary Begay and Grace Henderson Nez in 1974, when the price was $985. Resale price in 1996 is $3,000 to $5,000. 48 x 72 inches.* COURTESY HUBBELL TRADING POST

RIGHT: *This third phase chief blanket of handspun, predyed, processed wool by Elizabeth Kirk and Helen Davis is an old motif in a new weave. 48 x 48 inches.* COURTESY HUBBELL TRADING POST

elegance, enriched by a library of scarce Americana, and decorated with originals of famous Western painters.

The experience of a visitor to Hubbell's is one of participation, thanks to an arrangement by which the nonprofit Southwestern Parks and Monuments Association operates the trading post as an old-fashioned business. In addition to its regular customers, Hubbell's is visited by 180,000 tourists a year. The first trader at this historic site was Bill Young, followed by his son, John. Through the 1980s and into the 90s the post was operated by Bill Malone, who had been a trader two decades at Piñon. Malone had made Ganado a swapping center for old rugs, whose values, he says, have spiraled upward in recent years: "Where do I find them? They find me. People who inherit them from grandparents and don't appreciate them as native art bring them to me. They want to get rid of them, and I'm glad to oblige."

Malone was instrumental in putting together a most popular traveling exhibit, *Contemporary Navajo Weaving from Hubbell Trading Post*. The exhibit of twenty-six weavings meandered around Arizona under the sponsorship of the Arizona Commission on the Arts.

Working for hourly wages, two Navajo weavers—sometimes more—spend days recreating the original Hubbell rugs. They spin warp of Navajo wool, and weft from commercial skeins. Then, with antique rugs as models they weave duplicates, color by color, design by design. They faithfully repeat the individual flairs and flaws of the original weavers.

Don Lorenzo liked red. Generally he encouraged the weavers within his purview to limit themselves to natural tones: white, gray, and black. But the fashion of bayeta was established, so Hubbell made one concession to aniline dye, so long as it was red, a hue so strikingly rich, dark, and bold, it came to be called "Ganado Red." To heighten the dramatic impact of large areas of red, early Ganado weavers would also run their dark wool through aniline black.

The serrate, or stair-stepped diamond, came to dominate Ganado style. In some pieces one diamond is drawn out from end to end; in others three adjoining or interlocking diamonds fill most of the space. Don Lorenzo considered a rug design properly contained within borders, so the Ganado type often had a plain border of black or red, plus an inner border bearing

This Klagetoh by Grace Henderson Nez had a 1974 price of $3,000. 1996 resale price: $10,000 or more. 48 x 70 1/2 inches. COURTESY THE MUSEUM SHOP OF THE MUSEUM OF NORTHERN ARIZONA

a clean geometric repetition. Crosses, frets, triangles, zigzags, streaks, and chevrons are typical within areas unfilled by the Ganado diamonds.

Once Ganado was noted for its large rugs, and some big ones are still made. A Hubbell entry for the 1974 arts and crafts show of the Museum of Northern Arizona measured ten by fifteen feet. According to Gilbert Maxwell, a large Ganado, twenty-four by thirty-six feet, was made in four years by four weavers during the 1920s. A modern trend is toward smaller, refined weaves, some suitable for wall display. Quite a bit of white goes into traditional Ganado weaving, although some old pieces were sensational with just Ganado Red and dyed black.

The rug of the Kayenta area was once considered a regional type by authorities such as Maxwell. First cousin to the Ganado, it had a white background with one large diamond or several smaller ones in natural gray, intensified black, and aniline red, lacking the richness of Ganado Red. Borders often were doubled and undecorated. The central motif typically was serrated. When at the turn of the century Kayenta women were still struggling with borders, they tossed in a few extra end bands for good measure. This idea was carried over in some Kayenta weaving into recent times.

In the 1970s Bill Young could count at least one hundred superior weavers active in the Ganado sphere. Some of his favorites were Louise Begay, Grace Henderson Nez, Mary Begay, Faye Yazzie, Mary Amma Jones, Elsie Wilson, Sadie Curtis, Stella Toadachini, Yelthdezba Davis, Maggie Begay, Marie Begay, Esther Whipple, Annia Yazzie, Clara Jim, and Nellie Roan. Bill Malone in the 1990s would add Alice Balone, Mae Jim, Mary Baldwin, Barbara Tso, Freda Manymules, Alice Begay, Lena Begay, Gloria Begay, and Joanne James. Malone said never in modern times have there been more excellent weavers around Ganado than today.

Size alone came to distinguish the rugs of a group of weavers at Piñon to the north of Keams Canyon, very near the center of Navajoland. Large rugs are made there today. Kate Peck Kent tells of a long-ago example fifteen by thirty feet in size. Maxwell measured another that was fourteen by twenty-six. Borders, colors, and designs are pure Ganado: natural white, gray, and black; the black intensifies a red produced from aniline dyes. Few large weaves have been made in recent times, and the Keams Canyon classification is all but obsolete.

Positioned between the two areas where vegetal dyes are commercially successful, the weavers of Ganado are also turning to borderless tapestries in earth colors drawn from nature. The weavers of Klagetoh, once famous for Ganado-region rugs, have come under the influence of the vegetal dye revival at Wide Ruin, only ten miles to the south. Splendid contemporary Klagetoh weavers are Maxine Lee, Evelyn Yazzie, Elizabeth Bennally, Annie Tsosie, and Alice Begay.

The Ganado region of weaving extends to the east and southwest to include the communities of Cornfield, Sunrise Springs, Navajo Station, Lower Greasewood, and White Cone.

CRYSTAL

Within the wooded flanks of the Chuska Mountains, due north of the Navajo capital of Window Rock, perches Crystal, another trading post important to Navajo weaving. Crystal is outback, but like all other trading posts, it is more accessible today than in the past. From 1897 to 1911 J. B. Moore, the Crystal trader, educated scores of Navajo women in the weaving of rugs in styles that easterners presumed Indian patterns to be.

One tale has Moore obtaining a shipment of square-foot linoleum samples bearing patterns from Persian rugs. Moore issued the patterns, along with strong hints that he wouldn't buy anything else. Soon Moore's rug room was stacked with weaves done in a "genuine" Navajo design that would have fit on the floor of Omar Khayyam's tent. Strong borders, plain or fancy, were customary around mostly light-colored grounds. A strong central diamond extended into busy, doodlelike designs, most characteristically terminating in angular hooks resembling the letter G. Like Hubbell, Moore had no objection to red. He even shipped wool for refinement off the reservation, then supervised the dyeing at Crystal. Nearly all old-style Crystals contain red as well as white, gray, and brown-black.

Moore is thought to be the first to distribute a mail-order catalog of color illustrations of Navajo rugs. The finest Crystal weave in 1911, of about twenty-two square feet and weighing seven pounds, was priced at $20. Today a rare old Crystal in linoleum square pattern in best condition might be appraised at $10,000 to $30,000. After Moore gave up his trading post his influence continued for many years in the Crystal region.

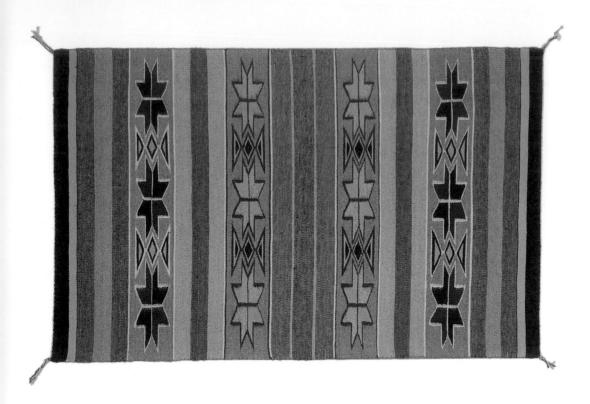

But renewed interest in weaving in the 1930s and 1940s involved vegetal dyes. Again today there is a Crystal-type regional rug, but it is radically different from the old Moore style. In the newer pieces there are no borders. Designs are edge-to-edge bands of earth colors, which seem extracted from a painted desert landscape. In a single weaving there may be rusty red, chocolate, natural gray, milky green, and a pastel vegetal pink. Within some bands are simple, geometric, repeated designs such as flat triangles, rhomboids, arrows, and stars. In wavy-line bands an illusion of motion is effected by alternating two or three wefts of contrasting colors.

Of all contemporary weaves, the Crystal type fits most quietly into mainstream home decor. Some present-day Crystal rugs are nearly square, but most are rectangular. The yarn is homespun, giving a nubby feel to the finished fabric. Two fine Crystal weavers of the 1970s were Mary Arthur and Faye C. George. Rivaling their work twenty years later are Priscilla Begay, Marjorie Hardy, Nanabah Harrison, Irene Clark, Sarah Begay, and Marie Brown.

A modern Crystal style tapestry by Mary Margaret Begay derives all of its colors from vegetal dyes. 36 x 56 inches. COURTESY THE JERRY AND LOIS JACKA COLLECTION

Two Grey Hills

Navajos have a way with names. One of their peaks is called Roof-Shaped Mountain on the Run. A sluggish stream is named Water Without Ambition. A place where wagons tended to bog down in sand is known as Where the Mexican Wept. On the east side of the reservation the two gray hills identifying the most refined and expensive textile of Navajoland are near a trading post of the same name, south of Beautiful Mountain and east of Flows into the Rocks Lake. In the Two Grey Hills region, including Toadlena and Tocito, sandstone and lava are sculpted into canyons and spires, and mountains rise to bear alpine conifers.

It was to this spectacular and isolated province that the patterns of J. B. Moore migrated eastward from Crystal, to evolve into one of the better-known and more prized Navajo textiles. Maxwell credits two competing traders, George Bloomfield and Ed Davies, with providing the motivation and instruction with which the weavers transformed their nondescript early rugs into the premium Navajo fabric by the mid-1920s. If so, these traders would have gotten nowhere without willing weavers who "kept their hands in the wool." Perhaps it is not accidental that quality weaving continued among Navajos far removed from the cultural shocks visited upon residents closer to roads and rails.

The Two Grey Hills rug of this day is a technical and artistic master-piece. Native wool in natural colors is intensively carded and spun as fine as thread. Weft counts of 120 to 150 per inch have been noted, as fine as cashmere and linen. By comparison, superior weaving elsewhere on the reservation may contain no more than 30 to 50 wefts per inch. Refinement of the Two Grey Hills type has been inversely proportionate to size. Rugs five feet by seven were about standard in the 1930s. Only well-to-do collectors can afford a weaving of that size today. Thus, many Two Grey Hills rugs are kept small, and are properly considered tapestries.

Colors are white, black, brown, tan, and gray. Subtle variations of shading are achieved by carding black with white, and brown with white. Within one rug as many as a half dozen tans may be manipulated. In a few rare examples bright colors have appeared, but because they did not sell well, the practice did not prevail.

By now, design has become so complex as to defy a general definition. Traditionally the outer border is dark, intensified by dye, in a plain band.

Inside this border is a second border of light ground, broken up with repeated geometric symbols: frets, squares, terraced chevrons, zigzags. Third and fourth border bands may mirror these themes in negative and positive treatment of color.

A favored motif of the enclosed rectangle is an elongated diamond, busily divided and extended by stair-stepped loops and hooks. Triangles and squares that fill out the rug corners sometimes refer to some aspect of the central diamond. Judges look for precise symmetry; when folded end to end or lengthwise, the halved patterns of better Two Grey Hills weaves will match nearly perfectly. Yet no two rugs are ever exactly alike.

This individual handling of each weaving within a regional convention is little appreciated off the reservation, yet it occurs today, and always has. With a little study a non-Indian can learn to recognize Navajo rugs. Gaining more knowledge he or she might identify a Navajo rug of the Two Grey Hills type. But the advanced student perceives the uniqueness of weave within each controlled creation. It is art.

In art museums Da Vincis and Rembrandts and Picassos are not thrown on the floor to be trampled by viewers. The works of masters are safely displayed and carefully lighted at eye level. Since the bulk of Navajo weaving was purchased for utility as well as beauty, America nationally tends to regard it as a quaint craft industry. Within too many institutions of natural history and anthropology artistic Navajo weavings are stored out of sight, emerging only for study as objects of culture or economy. One exception: under glass in the Denver Art Museum, a permanent place of honor is given to a tapestry by Daisy Taugelchee, artist.

About a hundred excellent weavers were producing Two Grey Hills tapestries during the 1970s. Recognized were Julia Jumbo, Mary Tom, Julia Theadore, Daisy Taugelchee, Mary Gilmore, Mildred Natoni, Mary Joe, Mary Louise Gould, and Elizabeth Mute. Of high repute today are Alice Gorman, Rachel and Melvin Curley, Ritah Bedah, Theresa Begay, Fannie Begay, and Virginia Deal.

CHINLE

Due north of Ganado on State Highway 63 Chinle sprawls at the mouth of Canyon de Chelly, a Navajo sanctuary. A national monument but still under Navajo ownership, Canyon de Chelly was the last refuge of Diné

during their times of greatest trouble. The canyon slashes a series of gorges into the red sandstone of the Defiance Plateau. Sheer, smooth walls rise nearly a thousand feet to surround monolithic spires taller than Manhattan skyscrapers. Ancient ruins cling to niches in the mineral-stained walls.

On the valley floor and beyond the mouth of the canyon Navajos dwell in old-style hogans and newer, square houses with turquoise-colored roofs. They cultivate vegetables and fruit and tend herds of sheep whose best wool is saved for the rugs of the Chinle region. Chinle weaving extends from Many Farms on the north to Nazlini on the south.

In the memory of oldtimers Chinle rugs were tightly packed and of generally good quality from the turn of the century to the 1930s. As for design, they were indistinguishable from rugs made throughout the reservation: black border, big central diamond in terraced red, gray, and black.

"I was in Chinle when the change took place," recalled the late Tom Kirk, of a large and highly regarded family of Indian traders. "Cozy McSparron and others at the Thunderbird Ranch encouraged the weavers to try soft, pastel colors and to weave in borderless designs with bands reaching from edge to edge. For awhile Cozy had a bunch of weavers making rugs this way, while across the hill, Garcia's trading post had them weaving the usual black-gray-red. In time, Cozy's idea won out."

Acceptance of the muted colors did not come easily. McSparron experimented with vegetal dyes, and Mary Cabot Wheelright inveigled the Du Pont Company to produce dyes in pastel shades for Navajo use. The Du Pont dyes proved to be unsatisfactory for use by unschooled weavers, but one of McSparron's concepts—edge-to-edge banding—revolutionized Chinle design.

Credited with giving Navajo women an array of practical vegetal dyes is Mrs. Nonabah G. Bryan. While teaching at Wingate school, Mrs. Bryan, a Navajo, tested numerous recipes for vegetal dyes during the 1930s. Classes at Wingate in the middle of that decade were instructed in their preparation and application. In 1940 Mrs. Bryan published a booklet detailing the formulas for eighty-four shades derived from organic and mineral materials native to Navajoland. The research has been advanced by others, notably Mabel Myers, also a Navajo, and today the formulas number in the hundreds. Tree bark, flower petals, bulb skins, wild carrots, pine needles, leaves, lichen, corn kernels, berries, cactus fruit, walnut shells—each source contributes its own hue from nature. Mordants to set the dyes include urine, raw alum, and juniper ashes.

At Chinle today many but not all weavers spin and dye their yarn. The weft is relatively coarse, and during weaving weft threads are not packed down hard. The result is a thick, textured rug. Some weavers incorporate the Crystal wavy-line weft treatment into band designs. Along with the earthen browns, yellows and reds, and the subtle greens and grays, Chinle weavers use some brighter aniline colors and a tasteful amount of white. Typically, in the same rug, groups of plain stripes will separate bands adorned with repeated, terraced diamonds.

Well known are the full-time Chinle weavers Isabell Johns, Ruth Ann Tracy, Helen Bia, and Marie and Grace Brown. But more typical is Vangie Jones, a younger weaver. Of a recent year she was holding down a regular

This Wide Ruin style creation by Marie C. Begay was a prizewinner in 1987. 35 x 49 inches. COURTESY THE MUSEUM OF NORTHERN ARIZONA

office job, going to college, and weaving in her spare hours. Meanwhile, her mother, Zonnie Jones, who could speak no English, worked her loom eight hours a day to make a living. Vangie said she could never weave full time, only as a hobby.

WIDE RUIN

Another region participating in the so-called vegetal revival surrounds the trading post of Wide Ruin, Burntwater, and Pine Springs. This land of cedar breaks, sandy water courses, and rolling roadways lies along the south-central border of Navajoland.

When, in 1938, Bill and Sallie Wagner Lippincott took over the Wide Ruin post, they induced their weavers to turn to colors extracted from nature and imparted to reservation grown wool. The Lippincotts refused to accept inferior weaving. They encouraged a return to old-style elements—

All vegetal dyes went into this Wide Ruin style weave by Bah Yazzie Ashley. 40 x 60 inches. COURTESY THE KILGORE COLLECTION

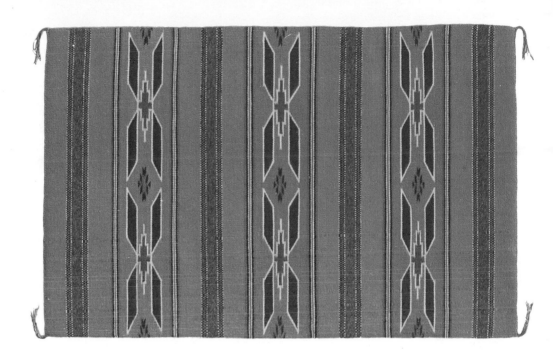

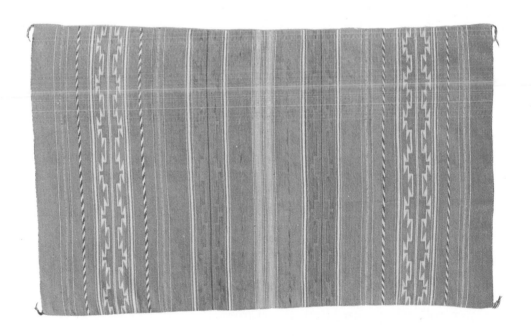

connected diamonds and triangles, lines of rhomboids, and alternating straight lines extending from edge to edge without a border.

Although some bordered tapestries nowadays are elaborations of patterns introduced by Hubbell at Ganado, the hundred excellent weavers of this region manufacture mostly borderless rugs.

The restrained ochre, sepia, and umber hues combined with muted blues and grays give weaves of this region a character of quiet dignity. In the 1970s noteworthy weavers of Wide Ruin-Burnt Water-Pine Springs were Ellen Smith, Lottie Thompson, Nellie Roan, Marjorie Spencer, Blanche Hale, Philomena Yazzie, and Maggie Price. More recently enjoying recognition are Annie Tsosie, Agnes Smith, Betty B. Roan, Mary Jane Baker, Virginia Ambrose, Cora Baldwin, Evelyn Yazzie, Alice Balone, Victoria Keoni, Helen Keoni, Helen Kirk, Virginia Yazzie, Jennie Thomas, and Celia Balone.

TEEC NOS POS

Northernmost of the Navajo weaving regions is Teec Nos Pos (Circle of Cottonwoods) near Four Corners, where Arizona, Utah, Colorado, and New Mexico join at a common point. (At a surveying monument it is possible for a visitor, on hands and knees, to occupy four states at once.) Only in recent times have paved roads penetrated the sweeping valleys and broken mesas of the San Juan River country. The weaving region encompasses the area around Teec Nos Pos, Arizona, and Beclabito, New Mexico. With energy-hungry municipalities drawing upon the rich reserves of oil, natural gas, and coal of Four Corners, the past two decades have brought wrenching change to Teec Nos Pos.

Yet enduring there is a kind of rug dating to the 1890s. The origin is lost, but that was a time when traders were aggressively converting weavers of blankets to weavers of rugs. As with J. B. Moore of Crystal, perhaps an early trader passed around pictures of the kinds of rugs then most fashionable in the homes of America. Undeniably, a lot of Persia appears in a Teec Nos Pos rug. The border is wide and lavishly decorated with repeated geometrics. Some central themes fall midway between old Crystal and new Two Grey Hills patterns. Other centers are flamboyant, interlocking diamonds. Amid hooked and forked zigzag lines Teec Nos Pos weavers will scatter stylized feathers and arrows.

Lively outlined colors seem to spring from the surface of this modern Teec Nos Pos tapestry by Bertha and Cora Tom. 62 x 84 1/2 inches. COURTESY GARLAND'S NAVAJO RUGS

Strong border treatment with dramatic use of dark background yarns enhance the power of this Teec Nos Pos creation by Tsosie Hyden. COURTESY THE KILGORE COLLECTION, SCOTTSDALE, ARIZONA

Busy and brilliant in out-line designs is this 1970 Teec Nos Pos tapestry by Esther Williams.
COURTESY THE READ
MULLAN COLLECTION

As if that weren't enough, the weaves are done in bold aniline-dyed handspun or commercial yarns. The trademark of a Teec Nos Pos weave is the outlining of each design element with a contrasting color. Somehow, as entities unto themselves, these garish hodge-podges can be quite appealing, but they blend with difficulty into home decoration.

Authorities disagree as to whether the women of Red Mesa, Sweetwater, and Mexican Water to the west of Teec Nos Pos constitute a separate region of weaving. In the past their designs and colors have been less gaudy and commercial. But as in Teec Nos Pos pieces, Red Mesa rugs boast of extra wide borders, centers with diamonds, and outlined designs.

Today weavers of note include Alice and Helen Begay, Mary Tom, Bessie George, Alice Nelson, Tsosie Hyden, Rena Yazzie, Evelyn Yazzie, Cora Whitney, Evelyn Poyer, Bertha Tom, Cora Tom, and Marie Wallace.

WESTERN RESERVATION

The region of weaving on the west side of Navajoland is as large as some eastern states. The region is roughly 120 by 50 miles, from Coppermine on the west to Chilchinbito on the east, from Kaibito on the north to Tuba City on the south. Other weaving centers in this region are Shonto, Inscription House, Kerley's Trading Post, Cameron, The Gap, Paiute Mesa, Navajo Mountain, and Cedar Ridge. For these far-flung communities Tuba City functions as something of a satellite capital.

Exciting innovation has bypassed the weaving of the western reservation. Prevailing styles date to the early 1900s—conventional geometric with borders in black, white, brown, and gray in natural tones, and aniline red. Vegetal dyes occasionally appear, but there seems to be no acceleration in this direction. No better saddle blanket is made than that of Inscription House.

The best-known, most easily recognizable pattern of this area is the Tuba City Storm, which is woven at other places besides Tuba City. No style has attracted more contradictory lore. One tale ascribes the origin to a pattern printed on sacks of flour shipped to western Navajoland in the early days. Then again, since J. B. Moore of Crystal, New Mexico, included a storm pattern in his 1911 catalog, it may have sprung from one of his patterns. Still another possible origin is from a Tonalea trader with a keen appreciation for what paleface rug buyers expected in the way of Indian symbolism.

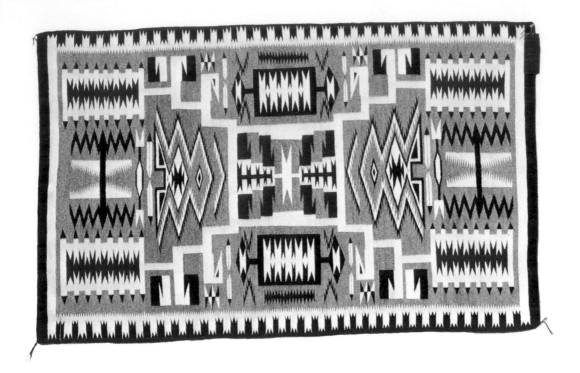

TOP LEFT: *Ella Yazzie Bia of White Clay, Arizona, was commissioned to copy a design in Read Mullan's catalog. In six months the job was done. 39 x 63 inches.* COURTESY THE TOM E. KIRK COLLECTION

BOTTOM LEFT: *Genesis of storm pattern elements are shown in this early example, circa 1910. 46 x 60 inches.* COURTESY THE MUSEUM OF NORTHERN ARIZONA

RIGHT: *The late Larry Yazzie's "Blue Canyon" raised outline style of weaving endures in this piece by his sister, Marilyn Scott. Detail shows three-dimensional surface of a typical raised outline weave. 30 x 60 inches.* COURTESY THE JERRY AND LOIS JACKA COLLECTION

Borders of storm patterns seem electrified by zigzags or contrasting steps. Against a usually gray background in the middle is an elaborate square, "the center of the world." In the four corners are smaller colored squares or rectangles, "the houses of the wind, the four sacred mountains." Strong zigzag lines, "lightning," join corner boxes with the center as if charging the entire rug with white, slashing thunderbolts. For an extra measure some storms include swastikas and stylized water beetles.

Weavers of note in this region are Mabel Bighorse, Marie Sheppard, Wanda Begody, Lilly Touchin, and Mary Wilson Begay.

COAL MINE MESA

Perhaps the most significant novelty in Navajo weaving in the 1970s gained first acceptance in the Coal Mine Mesa southeast of Tuba City. The technique is called raised outline, in which additional weft thread emphasizes the outlines of designs. The region has long been known for its skilled weavers of twilled saddle blankets and two-faced rugs, which display three-dimensional treatments of weft threads. The work today of Marilyn Scott, Marie Watson, and Jeane Begay is excellent. Gilbert Maxwell credits the

As if sizzling with electricity is this storm pattern by Rosa Dan Begay of Dinnebito. 33 x 52 inches. COURTESY BLAIR'S DINNEBITO TRADING POST, PAGE, ARIZONA

furtherance of raised-outline weaving to the late Dr. Ned Hatathli, a Navajo educator who served as the second president of Navajo Community College.

Weaving associated with the Coal Mine Mesa is in a state of flux, with the relocation of Navajo families southward to the vicinity of Sanders (New Lands style, page 76). But remaining in the Coal Mine Mesa area today are entrenched Navajo families who will be the most difficult to relocate. They indicate they will fiercely hold possession of their land; they may also express their defiance through continuation of the Coal Mine Mesa regional style.

GALLUP

Shape defines the primary weaving of the Gallup region, which reaches northeastward to Tohachi, Coyote Canyon, and Standing Rock in the northwestern corner of New Mexico. Long and narrow, the style has always been nicknamed a "throw," and in inferior examples, it deserves the additional word "away."

Many throws are coarsely woven on commercial cotton warps of bright commercial yarns in simple designs. Lacking a strong wool foundation,

This two-faced yei rug by Martha Tsosie is entirely of handspun yarn, 20 wefts per inch. 46 x 57 inches.
COURTESY THE RAY
GWILLIAM COLLECTION

these throws are not serviceable as saddle blankets or covers, or as rugs. They make chair backs and tablecloths and are relatively inexpensive.

Better throws, in the standard one-and-one-half-by-three-foot size, can be starkly handsome in black, white, gray, and red in balanced geometric patterns, or in abstract pictorials, such as corn stalks and ceremonial figures. Some of the old throws were woven extremely tight and, thus, command a premium price.

SHIPROCK

A volcanic neck rises 1,400 feet above the surrounding plain in the northeastern corner of the Navajo Reservation. An imaginative paleface dubbed it Shiprock. The Navajo people have another name for it: Winged Rock, on which the gods swept ancestral Navajos into the sky, out of reach of enemies.

This is one example of the Gallup throw rug. Homespun in natural white and aniline-dyed wool on cotton warp, the design is in red borders with black. 19 1/2 x 37 inches

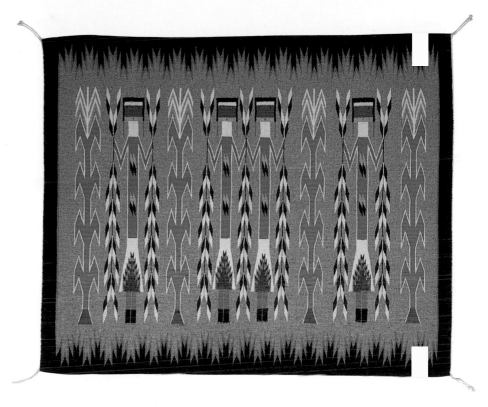

This Navajo yei weave by Mary Yazzie was a ribbon winner at the O'odham festival of the Gila River Reservation (Arizona).

In such a land of long shadows and mystical vibrations one would expect spirits to invade Navajo weaving. In the Shiprock region, they do, although again the medicine man was a white trader. It's said that just after the turn of the century Will Evans of the Shiprock Trading Company induced weavers of the region to portray *yeis*, the supernatural beings who communicate between the Navajos and their gods. From the town of Shiprock on the San Juan River, the weaving region extends southwestward toward Rattlesnake and Red Rock.

The Shiprock yei customarily has a white or light-colored ground. From three to six yei figures—tall and slender and bearing ceremonial appurtenances—face outward in stiff, upright postures. There may be a border; likely not. In more elaborate yei rugs three sides are marked off by the elongated body of a "rainbow goddess." The first yeis were woven in the face of tribal opposition, inasmuch as the figures are taken directly from sandpaintings crucial to sacred ceremonials. But since no religious significance was attached to the rugs themselves, opposition evaporated, and today there seems to be no objection to the manufacture of yeis. They are not used in Navajo worship; they are not prayer rugs.

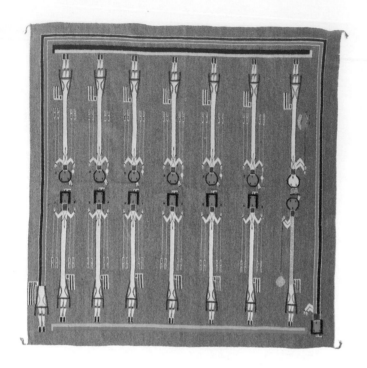

Large yeis have been made in the past, but the direction definitely is toward a size more suitable for hanging, about three by five feet. Much smaller and finely woven yeis have been produced in recent years, such as in the work of Betty Bia and Mary Burbank.

In a carryover from the turn-of-the-century Germantown color binge, Shiprock yeis take on bright, bold hues. Commercial yarns and aniline dyes are much in evidence, and within a single weaving a dozen or more colors may be used.

Markedly different from a yei rug is another design called *yeibichai*. A *yei* is a deity, and a yei rug depicts the spirits themselves. Navajo dancers in certain rites personify these spirits in the yeibichai dance. Thus, the rug that pictures dancers is the yeibichai type. The figures are more humanlike, and the action of the dance is commonly suggested by uplifted feet. In the 1970s weavers increased production of very small (some only one foot square) yeibichai tapestries in handspun, vegetal-dyed yarns for an attractive, understated style.

The popularity of these refined, yet affordable pieces grew from the combination of natural colors with recognizable Navajo symbolism. Yei and yeibichai weaving spread throughout the reservation. In the Navajo show in Flagstaff in 1974 ribbon winners were Helen Tsinnie of Tuba City and Leona Holiday of Rough Rock. Today prize yeis and yeibichais are done by such talented weavers as Marie Brown, Velma Begay, Della Woody, Marilyn Paytiano, and Mary Chase.

LUKACHUKAI

Another strong region of yei weaves is the region west of the Lukachukai Mountains around the trading post of that name and including Upper Greasewood and Round Rock.

Unlike Shiprock yeis, the rugs of Lukachukai tend to backgrounds of dark gray, black, tan, or even red. Multicolored yei figures are arranged in single or double rows. There may or may not be a border. Long noted as a region of handspun yarns, Lukachukai exports a true rug, thicker, nubbier, and coarser than the Shiprock counterpart. White, black, brown, green, blue, yellow, and red brighten the yei figures, and all but the white are, likely, aniline base. As with Shiprock weaves, sizes of Lukachukai rugs are becoming smaller. Today rugs with lifesize yei figures are rarely made.

This yeibichai pattern by Virginia Nakai shows both male and female dancers in a healing ceremony. 75 x 49 inches. COURTESY GARLAND'S NAVAJO RUGS

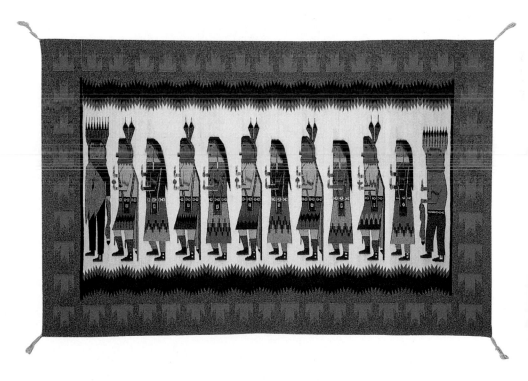

LEFT: *The modern Burntwater style is exemplified in this tapestry by Victoria Keoni.* COURTESY THE HEARD MUSEUM GIFT SHOP

TOP RIGHT: *Wanda Begay is one of the creators of the New Lands regional weave. This rug is done in Burntwater colors incorporating a Teec Nos Pos design, with the pattern emphasized by raised outline.* COURTESY THE KILGORE COLLECTION, SCOTTSDALE, AND R.B. BURNHAM TRADING POST, SANDERS, ARIZONA

BOTTOM RIGHT: *This contemporary weaving by the late Larry Yazzie represents the newest and most innovative form of Navajo woven art to date. He named his unique style Blue Canyon raised outline in honor of his homeland in the Coal Mine Mesa area from which his family was relocated. Wanda Begay, his sister, who taught him to weave, is credited with perfecting the New Lands style of weaving. Larry's rug contains abstract, geometric, and pictorial design elements; a corn stalk, feather, and bird in flight are framed by terraced cloud symbols. 32 x 62 inches*

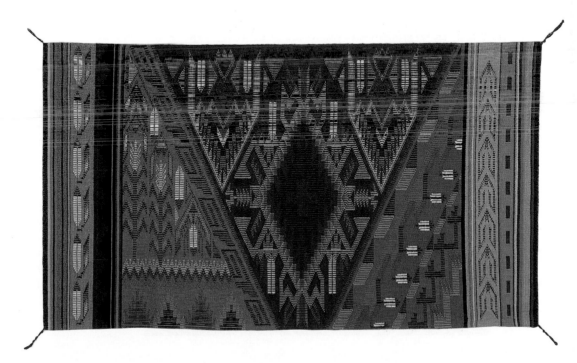

New Lands

The first new regional style in nearly four decades is emerging from yet another Navajo trauma. Hundreds of families, uprooted by a controversial federal relocation program of the 1980s, are expanding a community near Interstate 40 around the town of Sanders, Arizona, some twenty miles west of the New Mexico line. The relocation grew out of a dispute of land ownership between Navajo and Hopi tribes.

Bruce Burnham, fourth-generation trader, is credited with inspiring weavers relocated from Coal Mine Mesa to create the New Lands pattern—a hybrid, avant-garde fabric of fashionable pastels. The style employs raised outline to heighten the precision of patterns. The patterns bear some relationship to patterns seen in Teec Nos Pos weaves, but in muted coloration.

New Lands style gained almost overnight recognition when Wanda Begay took Best of Show at the 1987 Gallup Ceremonials, and won first place at the Museum of Northern Arizona's 1987 show.

Non-Regional Rugs

Twill Weaving

In many areas of Navajoland weavers produce twilled textiles. Numerous loom heddles are employed to manipulate the vertical warp cords to allow

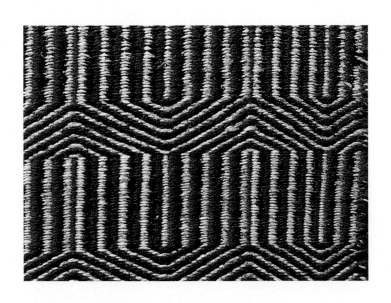

RIGHT: This thick twill weave in red and black is by Mary Anne Yazzie. Close-up photo (left) reveals complexity of stitches. 1974 price: $147; 1996 resale price: $450 to $500. 35 x 48 inches. COURTESY THE MUSEUM SHOP OF THE MUSEUM OF NORTHERN ARIZONA

weft threads to pass over and under unlike numbers of warps. Herringbones, diamonds, zigzags, and other geometric effects are achieved. The typical twill piece is limited to natural colors, although a bit of red sometimes appears. Twill weaving is sometimes called double weaving, in that one side mirrors the other in texture and pattern.

SADDLE BLANKETS

Native weavers once provided their families with ponchos, leggings, sashes, saddle girths, wearing blankets, door covers, and saddle blankets. Some sashes are still seen: Navajo women wear them under their silver concha belts to protect their velveteen blouses. But currently the only item manufactured for utility is the saddle blanket.

The size is standard. Ideally a single saddle blanket is about thirty inches square. The double saddle is roughly thirty inches by sixty. Quality

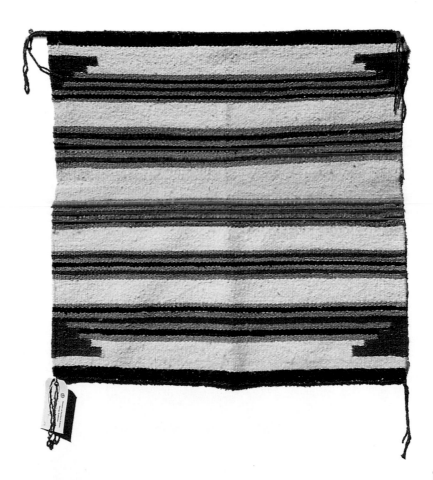

This typical single-saddle blanket of natural handspun is out of Blair's Dinnebito Trading Post. 31¹/₂ x 30¹/₂ inches. COURTESY THE MUSEUM OF NORTHERN ARIZONA

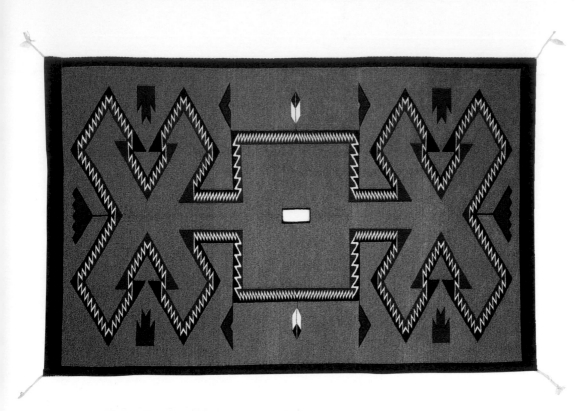

These hand-woven pillow covers by women at Sanders, Arizona, are gaining popularity through the encouragement of Bruce Burnham. COURTESY R.B. BURNHAM TRADING POST

of weaving can vary greatly. Many are coarsely woven and poorly shaped. Yet in top-grade saddle blankets some of the best of contemporary weaving is represented.

SPECIAL WEAVES

Certain weavers are willing to produce almost anything if the price is right. In the mid-1970s there began to appear at Hubbell's pictorial rugs in perfect perspective. One showed the trading post itself in three-dimensional proportion. And how did the weaver achieve perspective? Using her mind's eye as a photographic enlarger, she "blew up" a picture postcard scene of the structure. Into the 1990s a few weavers, such as Linda Nez, are crafting pictorials with rounded forms, unlike the zigzags delineating most pictorial forms.

In vogue for the 1990s are unusual shapes. Rose Owens is not the only weaver now making cross rugs, thirty-six inches square, for table covers. Alice Begay, when she weaves her thirty-six-inch-diameter round rug, uses

LEFT: This latter-day "Spider Woman" weave by Rena Mountain keeps faith with an old idea. In the center of the tapestry is "the hole where Spider Woman came through to teach us to weave." The practice was discouraged by early traders who believed (probably correctly) that such an opening in the fabric could be considered a flaw. Today, rare "Spider Woman" rugs are highly prized by collectors. 38 1/2 x 60 inches. COURTESY BLAIR'S DINNEBITO TRADING POST

Rainbow Bridge National Monument, hereford cattle, buckskin ponies, Navajo sheep, sheepherds, a sheep dog, and howling coyotes share space in this busy pictorial rug by Serar Tso. 48 x 51 1/2 inches. COURTESY BLAIR'S DINNEBITO TRADING POST

a wagon wheel as her loom. Anna Mae Tanner is a master of the four-in-one rug, in which four regional styles are incorporated into a single large weave. Another growing specialty are the miniature tapestries coming out of the Fort Defiance area. Bruce Burnham of Sanders in recent years has encouraged his weavers to produce pillow furniture covers.

Through the years women have woven the American flag, mottoes, landscapes, automobile emblems, optical illusions, and semaphores. Occasionally a superior weaver, such as Helen Scott, will revive an old-style chief pattern. Janet Tsinnie will do a brand-new Germantown eye-dazzler; Pauline Yazzie will weave an old-fashioned Ganado hall runner. There are women who still know how to produce a wedgeweave (sometimes called pulled warp weave), with bands stacked with oblique stripes. Because this type of weaving forces the warps out of the normal vertical pattern, the edges of wedgeweave rugs are wavy. Wedgeweave rugs dating to the 1890s are quite rare (see page 38).

This pictorial by Geanita Johns is something of a marriage of styles. Yeibichai dancers perform a healing ceremony for a Navajo audience. COURTESY TOH'ATIN GALLERY, DURANGO, COLORADO

Into the 1990s modern weavers have revived a century-old idea: the multiple pattern. In it are a variety of regional and technical types. Still young, although a weaver for twenty years, Minnie Yazzie of Teec Nos Pos will do fifteen different patterns on a plain white background. In complexity Minnie has a way to go to match the multipattern of Sarah Paul Begay: twenty-four rug styles of 130 colors.

Another unusual and expensive Navajo rug is the two-faced. Multiple heddles are required to produce dramatically differing designs on the two faces of a single rug—perhaps a yei pattern on one face, and an allover geometric or striped pattern on the reverse. Some weavers, as in the Chinle area, are so skilled they never look at the backside of their weaving, yet their patterns come out just right. In the 1970s Audry Wilson of Ganado and Mabel Burnside Myers of Pine Springs had reputations for two-faced weaving.

PICTORIAL RUGS

In the Southwestern textile collection of the Museum of Man in San Diego is a priceless pictorial rug, which exemplifies the wit, charm, and practical limitations of Navajo pictorial weaving. The representation is a Santa Fe train. Smoke billows from the locomotive. A caboose brings up the rear. Birds soar above, and tracks lie below. Between are Pullman cars. Apparently some informant only partially explained how paleface people traveled cross-country in sleeping cars. The berths are correctly positioned,

The American and Arizona flags, woven to commemorate the nation's bicentennial, were inspired by Bill Young and Dorothy Hubbell, long associated with Hubbell Trading Post.

upper and lower, but the passengers are shown sleeping standing up (see page 86).

No matter, it looks nice. Pictorials today may be of almost anything within view: jet airplanes, meteors, helicopters, domestic and wild animals, rodeo ropers. One popular theme is of a green cornstalk bearing birds, no two alike. Rugs of this kind from the Lukachukai area are usually of aniline-dyed homespun wool.

The tradition of picture weaving is longstanding. In the Charles G. Mull collection a pictorial dated 1880–90 shows two hogans, one horse, and thirteen letters of the alphabet.

This spritely bird pictorial is by Rena Mountain.
COURTESY GALLERY 10, SCOTTSDALE, ARIZONA

PHOTO BY JERRY JACKA

One horse, thirteen letters
of the English alphabet,
four hogans, and lightning
strokes are all elements of
the design in this 1880–90
rug, handspun in aniline
red, indigo blue, natural
white, and lavender in four-
ply Germantown. 41/43 x
68 inches. COURTESY THE
GIL MULL COLLECTION

Of his famous "Railroad Blanket" in 1892 George Wharton James wrote in Indian Blankets and Their Makers: "That weavers are influenced in their choice of design by their environment I have illustrated a score or more of times, but never more forcefully than by the weaver from whom I purchased the fantastic blanket pictured in colors. . . .

"This weaver's summer hogan was not far from a siding on the main line of the Santa Fe Railway, some fifty miles west of Gallup, New Mexico, over the state line in Arizona.

"One day after she had set up her loom, she was aroused from her thought by the arrival of a train going west. That immediately suggested to her that she attempt to reproduce the engine and train of cars in her blanket. The sun was glistening on the rails, and this effect she reproduced by alterations of white and blue. (Read from bottom up.) The train was of passenger coaches, and there was room on her loom for only two cars, and these of rather compressed dimensions. To denote that they were passenger cars she introduced two human figures in each. While this work was progressing certain birds appeared on the scene, together with two women, one walking east and one west. A 'light' engine also came traveling east, and as the sun happened to be shining upon it as it passed it had a bright, glistening appearance, so she represented it by weaving it in white, while the windows of the cab are picked out in dark blue. A large and small rain-cloud also appeared on the horizon and these are duly represented.

"After getting ready for the next panel and no train appearing, she pictured six flying birds alighting on the track and five walking female figures. A rain-cloud is at each end of the group of walkers. This panel is followed by one showing two engines together, going west, with flying birds and rain-clouds above them.

"The next panel shows a sleeping car. The remainder of the panel is made up of fleecy clouds, flying birds, and rain-clouds, while the last panel is her very effective representation of a poultry train going west." 27 x 47½ inches. COURTESY THE SAN DIEGO MUSEUM OF MAN

A new height in patriotic weaving was attained in 1976 when, as a bicentennial project, two Ganado weavers, Sadie Curtis and Mary Lee Begay, wove four-by-six-foot, 50-star American and Arizona state flags, respectively. After the flags proudly flew over public buildings, they were publicly auctioned—$4,000 for Old Glory, and $3,750 for the state flag.

Among excellent pictorial weavers today are Elain Bia, Linda Nez, Della Woody Begay, Desba Jake, Laura and Linda Nez, Betty Patterson, Pauline Glasses, Sadie Begay, Isabell John, Elizabeth Yazzie, Daisy Nockideneh, Sadie Ross, LaVerne Barber, and Evelyn Tunney.

SANDPAINTING BLANKETS

The Navajo religion remains a vital part of reservation life. Ceremonial rites are kept fresh for every eventuality, ever toward enhancing the harmony of humans with the natural world. At thirteen, Navajo girls experience the Womanhood Rite signifying their arrival at puberty. Warrior Navajos seek the Enemy Way Rite on return from battle; many a veteran of Vietnam passed through this traditional purification.

Certified healers, Navajo medicine men and women perform astounding feats of memory. One ceremonial consists of some five hundred songs, each a twelve-verse set. To orchestrate such a ceremonial, the medicine doctor must memorize the equivalent of an entire Wagnerian opera—the words, the music, the lighting, the directing, the scene painting, and the stage movements of all characters, not just in a general way, but in every detail. A medicine healer and apprentices may spend much of a day perfecting an intricate painting of colored sands and powders. At a climactic moment the patient is seated on the painting, and during the rite, the painting is destroyed. The term sandpainting is misleading. Many ingredients besides sand are used; crushed minerals, charcoal, cornmeal, pollen, and pulverized blossoms. Once blessed with holy corn pollen, a sandpainting within a ceremonial hogan becomes no less than a pictorial altar ritually empowered to give or take health, or life itself.

Thus, it required great courage for the first weavers to risk incurring the wrath of the gods by defying the rule that ceremonial pictures be destroyed. (Blindness and death were among the presumed punishments.) Joe Ben Wheat has written that sandpainting tapestries were woven for Richard Wetherill as early as 1896 at Chaco Canyon. Consensus history

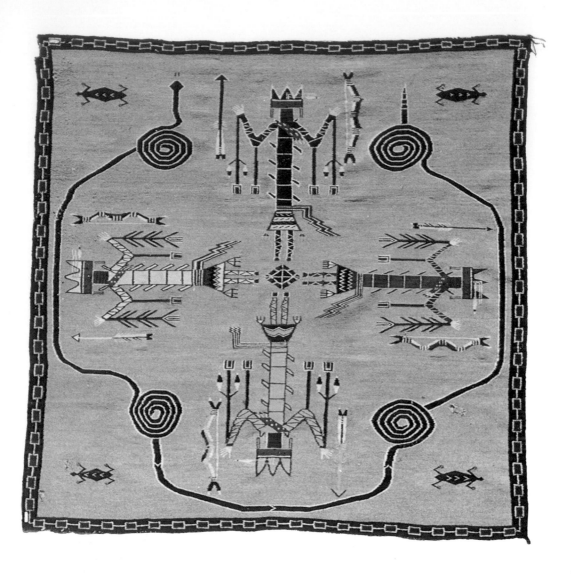

holds that in 1904 Hosteen Klah (Left-handed Singer) is believed to have woven about twenty ceremonial designs. He also helped in preserving drawings of sandpaintings, fortunately so, for today Navajo student doctors may inspect 650 sandpainting sketches preserved at the Museum of Navajo Ceremonial Art in Santa Fe.

So strong were early taboos, one weaver of a sandpainting blanket was forced by public opinion to take her weaving sixty miles away for sale. Another story relates that in 1906 a sandpainting blanket was secretly fashioned in a bolted back room of Simpson's Trading Post on Glayo Wash. No sooner was the blanket done than the weaver died, reinforcing fears and

This sandpainting weaving, collected in the early 1930s, features all hand-spun in natural white, natural wools combined as gray, black enhanced with dye, and the remaining yarns in aniline colors, eight warps and twenty-eight wefts per inch. 83 x 85 inches. COURTESY THE SAN DIEGO MUSEUM OF MAN

discouraging this kind of weaving. The rationale today is that if such a weaving is not quite completed (or deliberately altered from the actual sandpainting), blasphemy is avoided.

Such pieces by Klah are square. His, and those of other weavers, are usually patterned upon a tan background representing neutral sand. Yei figures, the "rainbow goddess," sacred plants, constellations, "earth mother and sky father," and numerous animal and storm symbols go into sandpainting weaving, which in the finest quality requires extraordinary weaving skills. As might be suspected, these weaves command huge prices. Award-winning weavers in the 1970s were Mary Song and Ruby Manuelito, who continues to weave. Currently outstanding makers of ceremonial blankets are two of Hosteen Klah's nieces, Gladys and Irene Manuelito, and Mary Long and Anna Mae Turner.

Within this Shooting Chant sandpainting style weave of Alberta Thomas is the theme of "The Buffalo That Never Die." 66 x 62 inches. COURTESY CRISTOF'S, SANTA FE, NEW MEXICO

The "Spirit Trail"

Much contradictory and confusing mythology has arisen regarding a thin line—sometimes mistaken for a flaw—which many women weave into the upper righthand corner of their rugs as they near completion. Most obvious are the lines that penetrate the border to the edge of the rug. These lines are of a contrasting color, usually of the inside background.

In basket and pottery designs such a break is of great antiquity in the Southwest. A host of explanations have been advanced, some by Indians, some by non-Indians. Traders tell believing customers the line is "the devil's highway," which "lets evil spirits out." Some weavers frankly admit they add the touch because their mothers told them to, and that buyers expect to find it. But otherwise it means nothing.

Clarifying the matter was a study pursued by Noël Bennett and published as "The Weaver's Pathway: A Clarification of the 'Spirit Trail'" in *Navajo Weaving*. Following a thorough search and numerous interviews with Navajo weavers, Ms. Bennett concludes that to most women the wefted gesture allows a pathway, so that a weaver's "spirit, mind, energies, and design" will not be trapped within the completed rug. In a sense the pathway line says, "May the next weaving be even better."

"The weaver's pathway" is a background color leading from an inner motif to the edge of the weaving.
COURTESY THE MUSEUM OF NORTHERN ARIZONA

7

Whither Navajo Weaving?

THE EVERLASTING STRENGTH of the Navajo people is their genius for adaptation. While other prehistoric American peoples vanished as tribal entities, Diné persevered. They bent to the hurricanes of change. They would not break. So today they are together, attaining self-determination, within their resource-rich refuge, stronger in numbers than ever before.

At a time when the artistic glory of long-vanished tribes lies faded and all but forgotten in museums, the jewelry, painting, ceramics, and weaving of Navajo artisans are acclaimed from coast to coast and around the world. Taken together, according to the U.S. Department of Commerce, Navajo arts and crafts today pump about fifteen million dollars annually into the tribal economy. Substantial numbers of those dollars come from Germany, Italy, England, Holland, and France, where Navajo handiwork became popular in interior design during the late 1980s.

White writers, who in their youth predicted the demise of Navajo weaving, have grown gray awaiting their dire forecasts to come true. Demand slowed somewhat in the economic recession of the early 1980s, but prices outgained the next round of prosperity. Many dealers agree that the market for Navajo weaving jumped to a new plateau around Christmas 1987. Such is the opinion of Dan Garland, whose gallery in Sedona, Arizona, routinely stocks five thousand Navajo weaves, said to be the largest inventory in the world.

Rivaling the brightness of yesterday's aniline-dyed yarns are these colors derived from natural resources such as plants and minerals by weaver D. Y. Begay.

"I believe at about that time a very large number of potential patrons came to look upon Navajo weaving as an emotional expression—not a quaint handcraft," says Garland. "When you touch a Navajo rug, you can feel the weaver in it. It came out of her heart and imagination. When you have one to keep, you know there is not another in the work like it.

"Good prize money at the shows is stimulating a quest for excellence. When superior items are made, they command as much as $60,000 or more—the selling price of a Two Grey Hills by Rosanne Lee Teller and Barbara Jeanne Teller Ornelles." This item, commissioned by Ed Fautz of Shiprock, New Mexico, took the women four years to fashion, with 108 to 125 weft threads to the inch. To achieve this tightness of weave, the yarn was carded for eight months, and spun to the thickness of dental floss. Subtle natural dyes included prickly pear cactus fruit and wild carrot. The claim was made that this weaving was the largest—five feet by eight feet, six inches—Navajo tapestry ever created. It won Best of Show at the Santa Fe Indian Market in 1987.

Meantime, prices for museum-quality older rugs march along in lockstep with freshly made weaves. Following is a casual sampler from Harmer Johnson's popular "Auction Block" feature in the quarterly magazine *American Indian Art:*

> *1980–81 auction season—Navajo man's serape, about seventy by forty-six inches, $54,000 (Sotheby's); Navajo child's serape, about fifty-one inches by thirty-four, $15,000; Navajo third phase chief's blanket, $11,500.*
>
> *1986–87 auction season—Navajo second phase chief's blanket, sixty-two by eighty-two inches, $33,000 (Skinner, Bolton); Navajo Germantown blanket, sixty-nine by twenty-seven inches, $27,000; Navajo yei, eleven feet eight inches square, $15,950.*
>
> *1988–89 auction season—Classic man's wearing blanket, forty-six by seventy inches, $93,000 (Sotheby's); Navajo late classic pictorial eye-dazzler, eighty-one by fifty-one inches, $35,200; Navajo transitional wedgeweave, forty-five by sixty-five inches, $8,800.*
>
> *1990–91—Early classic man's wearing blanket, $522,500 (Sotheby's); classic child's wearing blanket, $61,600 (Willis Henry's).*
>
> *1994–95—Classic chief's blanket, $41,400 (Skinner's); Germantown Moki, $9,200 (Channing's).*

These were among the top bids, to be sure, for the cream of the crop at the most prestigious auction houses. But the buying frenzy also enlivened sales in western cities, and at the auction of the estate of pop artist Andy Warhol, his favorite Navajo weaves fetched offers of five figures.

So old and new, the Navajo weaving market appreciates, in the view of some dealers, about 20 percent per year. It is still possible to find a passable Gallup throw for $100. But new "braggin'" weaves command thousands of dollars.

During the 1870s it was estimated that five thousand weavers were producing ten thousand items per year. Through the 1980s the number of capable weavers, according to some estimates, grew to twenty thousand with five thousand weaving full time. Production per capita did not double, however, because weavers increasingly work for wages on and off the reservation. Yet certainly weaving skills are not on the wane.

Some authorities believe that in quality the best of today compares favorably with the best of the Classic Period of the late 1800s. Indeed some admirers suggest that weaving was never so good. For such a resilient and renewable art, who dares to foretell its disappearance?

True, powerful forces contrary to the weaving tradition are at large. Electronics plants, sawmills, power generating stations, recreation enterprises, and service businesses are paying better wages. New supermarkets sell everything including mutton in Window Rock, Chinle, and Tuba City. Why weave with wool at home for pennies an hour, when wiring transistors can earn the money for fast food at the deli?

Weaving was once taught in schools. The courses were abolished during the 1950s and 1960s, and whereas some revivals in this training emerged in the 1970s, generally speaking the weaving art is not formally taught in classes. An exception is Navajo Community College at Tsaile, where weavers such as Mabel Burnside Myers pioneered in instructing classes as large as sixty aspiring artisans.

World markets newly compete for wool in bulk. In recent years great quantities of Navajo wool were sold to Japan. The close relationship once prospering between trading post operator and weaver is also going through change. In recent years some fifty reservation trading posts were shut down or converted to chain convenience stores. Surviving posts today are like town stores; self-service, no barter, no credit, cash and carry.

Taking up the financial slack are individual patrons who might commission a work. Galleries will also provide grubstakes to better weavers, to ensure a quality supply. It is not unusual for a modern mobile trader to keep twenty or even a hundred weavers on the string. Such an entrepreneur is Steve Getzwiller, who crisscrosses the reservation to make periodic payments and monitor the pieces he has contracted. Through a Scottsdale gallery, works of this sort of origin have found their way to the homes and collections of Ralph Lauren, Dick Cavett, and Walter Annenberg, and corporate offices as far off as Abu Dhabi.

The pickup truck has replaced the horse-drawn wagon. A weaver of Chinle can go to Gallup in less than two hours. Her prize-winning rug at the annual Indian Ceremonial is analyzed by weavers who live at Dinnebito, Dinnehotsa, and Tse Bonito, who also gadabout in pickup trucks. Regional ideas are freely swapped, slyly borrowed, and baldly pilfered.

Is this to be decried? What is traditional? If Navajos entering the Southwest followed tradition (insist archaeologists), they would not have taken up weaving at all. If the first traditions of Navajo weavers prevailed today, there would be no patterns other than quiet stripes, edge to edge. Did bayeta finalize tradition? Or the Germantown eye-dazzler? Or handspun? Or aniline? Or vegetal? Has tradition peaked with that stepchild of

Although modern homes, stores, and work places have come to Navajoland, many citizens continue to live at least part of the year in a hogan such as this—the traditional, many-sided, circular great room of timbers and clay.

the Middle East, the Two Grey Hills? Or is ceremonial sandpainting the final word? Or the abstract sculpted in raised outline from Coal Mine Mesa?

Unquestionably, Navajo weaving will undergo further change, and one possibility is a decline. The more optimistic view is that the art is on the threshold of widespread public acceptance for what it is—an art form. The experience of Southwestern Indian potters over the past three decades is most heartening. For centuries these potters clung to their ancestral techniques and designs while exploring fresh ways of emotional expression. They kept their art alive in a country accustomed to buying ceramics cheap, be they shaped in a factory or on a wheel. Abruptly, in the late 1960s and early 1970s, artistic values were recognized, and almost overnight the jewel-like, hand-burnished, manure-fired creations of certain Rio Grande Valley pottery makers were selling for thousands of dollars.

Compensation for most weavers remains inadequate but it is improving. As recently as the 1960s weavers were working for fifteen cents an hour. By the mid-1970s the labor investment required to create a three-by-five-foot vegetal-dyed rug was 388 hours from shearing through weaving. The greatest time-consumers were carding (40 hours), spinning (90 hours), and weaving (190 hours). If the rug at wholesale sold for $500, the weaver earned $1.30 per hour. Today weavers are yet to average minimum wage, but in a land of much unemployment and underemployment, a cash skill is doubly valuable. Al Packard, lifelong dealer in Indian arts and crafts in Santa Fe, put it into perspective: "If the weaver's income hadn't increased tremendously, there would be few, if any rugs on the market today."

Patrons of San Ildefonso pottery do not pay three thousand to six thousand dollars for vessels to be used as flower vases. As for weaving, Packard added, "If the rug buyer looks at a Navajo rug simply as floor covering, he should go to the chain store."

8

A Buyer's Guide to Navajo Weaving

SMALL COMFORT to the casual admirer of the art of Navajo looms, not even men and women who have devoted all their lives to such weavings see eye to eye. One trader who had in a long career turned over millions of dollars worth of Navajo textiles and had judged at the best of shows, told a story:

> There were four of us judging at a show one year. The scholar among us took a traditional point of view. Our anthropologist was interested in the cultural aspects. We also had an authority on sheep husbandry, and he concentrated on the quality of the wool. My interest was in design.
>
> And we never agreed on one damned thing.

It makes one wish, regarding wealth and circumstance, one were William Randolph Hearst. Thanks to a fluke of time and transportation, he lived the rug collector's dream. Hearst was obliged to travel often by train. Frequently the publishing mogul stayed the night in Albuquerque and shopped at the Fred Harvey store. From the late 1880s through 1920 he amassed a collection of two hundred pieces, now part of the Natural History Museum of Los Angeles County, from which, of a recent summer, was selected a traveling exhibit.

Some of the most beautiful and unique Navajo weaves are displayed for sale at the Museum of Northern Arizona's annual Navajo Craftsman Show.

The Hearst assemblage of fine old rugs is appraised today in the millions. But rugs are not all valuable because they are old. Plenty are just bad, old rugs. The buyer of elderly merchandise is well advised to research history and consult a respected dealer before spending hundreds or thousands of dollars for an obviously well-worn and clumsily made, faded piece represented as a "classic bayeta," or a "Bosque Redondo transitional" or a "Navajo Moki woven for trade with the Pueblo Indians." Unless documented data accompany such claims, doubt nags. Museum curators confess that unassailable conclusions are rare indeed.

Yet at one California auction in 1974, where old weavings were briskly selling for $300 to $7,500, the catalog contained numerous errors and exaggerations—however innocent, one cannot say. Ten years later a man at an eastside Phoenix, Arizona, swap meet purchased for $20 a textile represented as a saddle blanket. An expert appraisal identified a child's classic period wearing blanket in a condition worth (today) $1,500. The best policy for sellers and buyers of old rugs is to become knowledgeable or hire the services of a professional. Leads to local appraisers usually can be obtained from museums or long-established shops. As in any other calling, appraisers vary in skills.

The risk is less for investors in contemporary weaving. Quality, value, and provenance are more easily established for fresh fabrications. A laudable custom has caught on—the attaching to each item with sealed wire a price tag bearing information about the weaver, her design, and her home. The buyer of such a well-documented piece should leave the tag on the tapestry. Tucked out of sight for display, the tag can be invaluable at the time of resale.

It is pointless to seek precise standards in assessing Navajo weaves. The charm and challenge of the art form is its individualism. Appreciation of a particular work my be further blurred by that intangible element called taste.

Once, an Indian trader with fifty years' experience took an order for a hundred saddle blankets from a New York riding club. The specifications: the weaves were to be pure white and nothing but white, all exactly thirty inches square. The trader enlisted a score of weavers in the project. In three years the blankets were done.

"Few of them were square," he recalled. "The weaves varied, and many of them were embellished with little designs tucked off in the corners or along the edges. I was almost afraid to ship the blankets, but I did, and luckily the club members were delighted with another example of Navajo individuality."

This same trader noted that the popularity of certain designs stimulates production. But the public's desires may change. There is no guarantee that the sensation of today will be in high esteem tomorrow. The general rule for all art collection also applies to Navajo rugs. Buy what you like and will enjoy for a long time. That sort of dividend can carry an owner across fluctuations in monetary value.

Some of the guidelines for buying Navajo weaves are those that pertain to all transactions. Deal with dependable, established traders. Get a receipt that describes the merchandise. If today's purchase proves to be less than represented, will the dealer be reachable tomorrow? Beyond that:

- When assessing a rug, open it fully and lay it out flat. If rugs have been folded and stacked for a long time, they may have temporary wrinkles or creases.
- Only by surveying a weaving in its entirety on both sides can a buyer be sure there are no serious flaws and that edges are parallel, straight, and square at the corners. The corners should not curl.
- Fold the weaving lengthwise and widthwise to ensure that opposite sides are the same, or nearly so. Any variance (except on purpose, as in the two-faced rugs) is a serious flaw.
- Is the weave the same thickness throughout? Quality work can be coarse or fine, but it is always constant.
- Warp threads should not show through. If they do, something went wrong in the weaving. The loom lost its tension, perhaps, or the weaver was a novice.
- A knowing buyer will separate weft threads with a fingernail to determine the type of warp. A weave built upon cotton warp will not bear rough use as a floor covering.
- No Navajo textile is perfect. Slight imperfections or personal flourishes are acceptable so long as they do not diminish the structural integrity or detract from the overall execution.
- Colors should be uniform, especially within design elements. Variations in hue of patches of background weft come from careless dyeing and carding.

- Tightness and consistency of the weave is detected most surely by feel.
- Mexican, Oriental, and European imitations plague markets in Navajo weaves. The odor of sheep is often present in Navajo handspun works and is absent in counterfeits. Of course, the smell of sheep is also lacking in Navajo weaves employing commercial yarns.
- Rugs imported from Mexico in recent decades, although done in designs suggestive of Navajo weaves, are light to the touch, because lanolin was removed during commercial cleaning of the wool.
- The Navajo vertical loom, imparting great tension to the foundation cords during weaving, produces a tightly packed textile. Imitations from Mexico, woven on horizontal looms operated mechanically, are looser both of warp and weft.
- "Lazy lines" are commonly found in excellent weaves. These diagonal lines in the material occur where the weaver stacked several inches of weft. The lines are considered to be normal.
- If you cannot tell which end was the beginning, or which end was the completion, you are holding a quality item.
- Navajo edge warps are usually single, buttressed by edging cords. Mexican edge warps are commonly multiple and not reinforced with edging cords. The clues are not hard and fast. Some Navajo saddle blankets contain double edge warps. Imitators are said to be adding edging cords to their copies.

WHERE TO BUY?

Dealers of high repute can be found in all large cities of Arizona, New Mexico, Colorado, Utah, and California. In smaller communities an Indian trader may have earned the status of prideful, local institution. To name just a few: Garland's in Sedona, Arizona; Galeria Capistrano in San Juan Capistrano, California; Notah-Dineh Trading Company, Cortez, Colorado; Cameron Trading Post, south of Grand Canyon, Arizona; Charles Eagle Plume, Estes Park, Colorado; Gallery 10, House of the Six Directions, Margaret Kilgore, and Lovena Ohl, all of Scottsdale, Arizona; Bahti Indian Arts, Tucson, Arizona; and James Reid, Ltd., Cristof's, and Packard's, all of

Santa Fe, New Mexico. These are but one man's favorites. For guidance to other reputable dealers, write the Indian Arts and Crafts Board, U.S. Department of Interior, 1801 "C" Street N.W., Washington, DC 20240.

The Navajo people jealously guard the reputation of their arts and crafts enterprise based at Window Rock, Arizona. The enterprise operates branch shops throughout the reservation.

Tribally sponsored auctions attract bargain-hunters. At places like Crownpoint, New Mexico, auctions are held every couple of months throughout the year. Only ten percent of the gross revenue at Crownpoint goes to administrative overhead, so bargains abound for the knowing bidder. Typically about two hundred items are sold each selling day. Other auctions occur at Shiprock, New Mexico; Window Rock, Arizona; and the Heard Museum, Phoenix. At the Heard, a bonus may be a weaving demonstration by a talented Navajo, such as Nanaba Aragon.

On any given day the gift shop at the Heard offers weaving of dependable quality. In Flagstaff a tradition of excellence in Navajo goods continues at the Museum of Northern Arizona gift shop. Also, a large inventory of Navajo rugs is maintained at the Denver Museum of Natural History. Splendid examples of weaving are entered for judging and sale at the annual Navajo Show sponsored by the Museum of Northern Arizona.

The ultimate for the advanced collector is to commission a weaver to produce a custom weaving. This may call for partial payment up front on a handshake agreement. It is not an arrangement for those uncomfortable with the words faith and trust, and don't expect the finished item to be exactly as imagined.

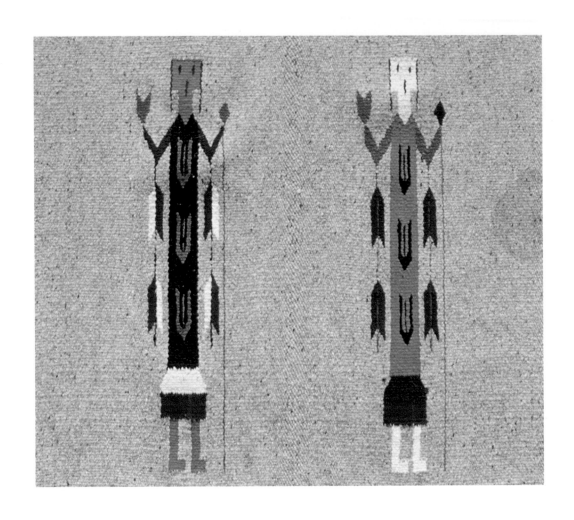

9

Fakes, Frauds, and Foolishness

IN 1957 Editha L. Watson, in an *Arizona Highways* magazine article, gave reassurance that Navajo weaving was beyond counterfeiting. "An attempt was once made," she wrote, "to counterfeit Navajo weaving, when an eastern firm tried to promote a line of machine-made 'Navajo' rugs. They might have known what would happen: traders and storekeepers bristled indignantly and refused every attempt to sell such merchandise. Certainly no one offered to buy it. The firm was forced to call in its samples and write the experiment off as a complete loss."

If once the commerce in Indian arts and crafts was so pure, it no longer is today. Concurrent with growing popularity and rising prices in genuine Indian goods, the traffic in imitation and fraudulent wares has also increased. Hand weaving, long considered invulnerable, is today competing in a world where machine-made imported rugs are foisted off on gullible customers as being of Indian origin.

Sales of Mexican textiles in tourist stores during the 1970s reached such proportions that the consumer fraud division of the Arizona Attorney General's Office took action. The legislatures of both Arizona and New Mexico made it unlawful to sell such products as Indian-made. But problems persisted.

For example, a slick national women's magazine continued to advertise: "Navajo. Try an American Indian pattern rug woven of dense, natural yarn in earthtone accents on ivory background of brick reds and golds . . . 4 by 6 feet, $39.95." The ad did not explain that this rug was a copy of a Ganado pattern and was imported from Belgium!

Even when clearly labeled as such, imitation rugs harm Navajo weavers. As *The Indian Trader* pointed out, "It should be noted that much good weaving is done in Mexico. When done honestly in the regional and tribal styles of the weavers it is well worth purchasing. Navajo rugs, however, sold at prices well below those commanded by authentic Navajo textiles, will only give Navajo weaving unfair competition and undermine the public's confidence."

Particularly handsome is another American-made textile, called the Chimayo, after a village in northern New Mexico. Sixth-, seventh- and eighth-generation weavers of Spanish descent produce serapes and blankets on looms centuries old. These horizontal looms are operated by a foot treadle. They quickly weave commercial yarn with a flying shuttle. Lovely as they may be, Chimayo weaves are no more Navajo than Pendletons.

Not all of the bad business deals are intentional. Traders can't be expert in everything, and some imitations are difficult to tell from the real thing. Nor are all the villains non-Indians. Some traders have claimed that Navajos have delivered Mexican imitations to their stores. According to another report, during the 1970s some thirty to forty horizontal, Mexican-type looms were obtained by Navajo weavers on the reservation. This development was doubly ironic—the abandonment of distinctive Navajo weaving in favor of the manufacture of Navajo copies of Mexican imitations of genuine Navajo weaves!

Along with the rise in monetary value of Navajo weaving and other native arts has occurred in an alarming increase in theft and burglary. Museums, trading posts, city stores, and private homes have become targets of professional criminals. The loot, much of it without identifying marks, has been sold through fences from Los Angeles to El Paso, for distribution as far away as Europe. So serious was the rise in crimes related to Indian arts and crafts (a rate of 90 percent a year was one estimate), that in 1974 the Indian Arts and Crafts Association was founded, based at Gallup, New Mexico. Among their goals was the registration, by serial number, of valuable items, and a national communications system for alerting dealers, collectors, craftsmen, and museums regarding stolen goods.

Similar schemes are advanced from time to time, most recently by the Navajo Arts and Crafts Enterprises with headquarters in the Navajo capital, Window Rock, Arizona. Navajo weaving would be authenticated with a piece of metal, stamped with a copyright mark, and permanently affixed with a seal to the fabric. As explained by a proponent, "It would identify the store that guarantees it as genuine. It would carry the date of registry, and it would have an exclusive serial number. This would be backed up with a detailed history of the item tied into the registry number in protected records so that a buyer could at any time in the future obtain the name of the weaver and other pertinent history."

Until some foolproof means of identity is perfected, the rule remains *caveat emptor*. That's not a Navajo phrase, but it does apply.

10

The Care and Feeding
of a Navajo Weave

AN ARTISTIC Navajo rug, blanket, or wall tapestry will last for generations if given proper care. The inherent ruggedness of Navajo weaving was demonstrated at the Chicago World's Fair when 2.8 million people walked across a rug without wearing it through. That was an old style weave of handspun reservation wool, heavy with lanolin, which lubricated the strands against the shock of footsteps and the grinding action of dirt. Rugs dating back to 1910 survive intact on busy aisles of schools and churches across the Southwest.

The treatment is not recommended for fabrics of recent manufacture. Most modern weaves of wool diminished in oils in refining processes do not have the resiliency of the older rugs. Even those proved vulnerable to the peculiar dangers imposed upon a textile spread upon a floor. Dogs gnawed off corners. Cats sharpened their claws. Plumbing leaked. Table and chair legs bored holes. When cocktails, food, and coffee were spilled, the rugs caught the outfall. Grit inevitably was tracked in on shoes. Sunlight streaming through windows unevenly faded colors. Finally, no matter how good the wool or weave, some wear occurred.

The trend of moving Navajo textiles from the floor to the wall solves most of these problems. But it also creates another problem that, until the advent of the space age, seemingly had no satisfactory answer. In short, how do you hang a tapestry without hurting it? Nails, tacks, and staples are subject to rusting, which stains wool. Any system of attachment that distributes weight to a series of fasteners tends in time to cut through strands.

Navajo weaves serve not only as floor rugs but also as furniture covers and wall art in this tastefully decorated great room of a Phoenix collector.

The Denver Art Museum curators hit upon a method of sewing the top edge of a wall display with clear monofilament (such as fishing line) to a wooden slat, which in turn is affixed to the wall. While the monofilament is nearly invisible, and weight is evenly carried by the slat, the large stitches impart an unbecoming scallop to the top border.

The ideal alternative grew out of a new system of fabric closure publicized by use in space suits for astronauts. One side of a garment opening would be fitted with a thin strip consisting of a myriad of tiny plastic hooks; the other side, a strip of nappy material. Now commonly used in parkas, knapsacks, sports uniforms, swimming suits, and gowns, the product is marketed under the trade name Velcro. Various widths now are sold in yardage goods stores.

Particularly convenient is a two-inch-wide strip of plastic hooks whose back side is precoated with contact adhesive protected by a paper shield. In use, the Velcro is measured and cut to length, the paper shield is removed from the backing, and the strip is pressed along a level line at a height where the weaving is simply pushed onto the hooked strip. Making adjustments to even borders and remove kinks is easy. Scraps of Velcro can be added here and there to flatten the whole weave against a wall.

When it is time to turn or clean, the weaving can be gently pulled off the hooks, no harm done. A Velcro-equipped photographic rack has held hundreds of Navajo rugs, new and old, and the Velcro strip acquired only a few stray fibers. One caution: the strip becomes a semipermanent installation. Removal destroys the Velcro and requires refinishing of the wall. As a courtesy Velcro is sold by the linear foot to buyers of rugs at many trading posts and galleries.

Museum curators go to extraordinary lengths to protect specimens, especially those of organic matter, of which a Navajo rug is 100 percent. The curator's manual, titled *Conservation: Navajo Rugs,* was written by Bob Morgan and Jeanne Brako and published in the summer 1987 edition of *American Indian Art* magazine. Excellent professional guidance is offered by Frederick J. Dockstader in his book, *Weaving Arts of the North American Indian.* Yet another resource is the booklet, *Velcro Support System for Textiles,* Canadian Conservation Institute, 1030 Innes Road, Ottawa, Canada K1A 0M8.

But the private owner of one or more Navajo textiles faces a simpler dilemma: how visually to enjoy the weaves, while providing reasonable protection against damage? Locking them away in a closely controlled storage environment is seldom an option for the casual owner.

Thus, compromising certain museum procedures, here are some practical tips for home care of Navajo tapestries.

- Never, never try to shake out dirt. The whipsnap action breaks fibers and loosens the corner knots.
- If a rug must go on the floor, use a foam mat underneath to prevent wear and skidding. Don't rest furniture legs on a Navajo rug.
- Try to maintain an interior climate around 70 degrees. High humidity and high heat are harmful over time.
- For floor use, avoid high traffic areas. Rotate for even wear.
- Vacuum cleaning is recommended as regular maintenance of floor-displayed rugs.
- Hang tapestries the direction they were woven. The up side is usually where the "weaver's pathway" occurs.
- Keep weavings away from ducts and sunlight.
- Moths are persistent and perfidious. Whether placed on the floor or wall, wool weavings should be turned at least twice a year. Some experts advise a twice-yearly spray with moth repellent. Others swear by spring and autumn exposure to a few hours of sunlight.
- Fumigant procedures call for forty-eight hours of exposure in a closed area. Museum experts do not recommend storage with moth balls, which may affect dyes.
- Navajo wool should never be washed in a machine with soap or detergent and water. Hand washing with soap and cold water might work well, but only after thorough testing to ensure the dyes will not run. A rug can be ruined by washing.
- Nearly every city of size and some small towns in the Southwest have at least one quality dry cleaner that specializes in Navajo and other native weaves. As often as not lanolin restoration and moth-proofing are parts of the process.
- For long-term storage, small weaves may be placed flat in a drawer,

separated by acid-free paper. Larger pieces can be rolled on carpet rollers covered with acid-free paper. Don't leave Navajo weaves folded for a long time. They'll develop lumps and permanent creases.

❖ Curling corners may be flattened by untying the corner knots and working a bit of yarn into the weave. Have an expert do it if you may not remember how to retie the knot.

Even museums and serious collectors are sometimes stumped by the puzzle of what to do with a damaged rug. Broken edge yarns can possibly be repaired by a patient amateur, but run dye, faded colors, and internal breaks of weft and warp call for a skill of weaving equal or superior to the original. Not many repair persons have the talent and dedication to accept such a challenge. Yet restoration is becoming more and more an acceptable procedure. The most desirable results are achieved when the reweaving is done expertly with materials consistent with the undamaged weave. Noël Bennett has established a center for the restoration of old Navajo textiles at Corrales, New Mexico.

Museums and collectors may know of other repair experts. Likely they are far behind in orders, despite the high costs for their labors. Some wrecked weaves, as with used cars, are not worth the price of repair. Reputable repair men and women will not take on work that will not result in a worthwhile finished specimen. In effect this limits repair to tapestries of great intrinsic value by virtue of rarity, style, or execution.

Selected Readings

Amsden, Charles. *Navajo Weaving*. 4th ed. Glorieta, New Mexico: Rio Grande Press, 1974.

Bennett, Noël. *Are You Sure?* Window Rock, Arizona: The Navajo Tribe and the Museum of Navajo Ceremonial Art, 1973.

———. "The Weaver's Pathway: A Clarification of the 'Spirit Trail'." In *Navajo Weaving*. Flagstaff, Arizona: Northland Press, 1973.

Bryan, Nonanabah G., and Stella Young. *Navajo Native Dyes*, no. 2, Education Division, U.S. Bureau of Indian Affairs, Lawrence, Kansas, 1940.

Dedera, Don, Katina Simmons, Carol Stout, Mike Noel, and Tony Hillerman, "Navajo Rug Special." *New Mexico Magazine,* February 1976.

Dockstader, Frederick J, *Weaving Arts of the North American Indians*. New York: Thomas Y. Crowell, 1978.

Elmer, Wilma. *Navajo Rugs*. Scottsdale, Arizona: Carlos H. Elmer, 1980.

Getzwiller, Steve. *The Fine Art of Navajo Weaving*. Tucson, Arizona: Ray Manley, 1984.

Iverson, Peter. *The Navajo Nation*. Albuquerque, New Mexico: University of New Mexico Press, 1981.

Jacka, Jerry, and Lois Essary Jacka, "The New Individualists: A Spectacular Journey Through the Realm of Native American Fine Art." *Arizona Highways,* May 1986.

———. *Beyond Tradition: Contemporary Indian Art and Its Evolution.* Flagstaff, Arizona: Northland Publishing, 1988.

———. *Enduring Traditions: Art of the Navajo.* Flagstaff, Arizona: Northland Publishing, 1994.

Kent, Kate Peck. *Navajo Weaving.* Phoenix, Arizona: the Heard Museum, 1961.

Maxwell, Gilbert. *Navajo Rugs: Past, Present and Future.* Palm Desert, California: Desert Southwest Publishing, 1948.

Merry, E. S. "So You Want to Buy a Navajo Rug?" Gallup, New Mexico: The Inter-Tribal Indian Ceremonial Association, 1972.

Wheat, Joe Ben. "Three Centuries of Navajo Weaving," *Arizona Highways,* July 1974.

Acknowledgments

IN THE RESEARCH AND PREPARATION of this book thanks are due to the San Diego Museum of Man and the Museum of Northern Arizona at Flagstaff, which opened up their extensive collections for examination and photography. The courtesies of Stefani Salkeld, Helen Turner, and Barton Wright were especially helpful. Gratitude is extended also to Tom E. Kirk, Martin Link, Charles G. Mull, Bill Young, and Clay Lockett for their insights into contemporary Navajo weaving. Herb and Dorothy McLaughlin generously provided many photographs from the considerable stock of Arizona Photographic Associates, and where weavings from private collections are pictured, the owners are credited, with thanks.

For the first edition of this book about a native textile, the most important Weaver is one named Paul, whose Northland Press against all odds has established the nation's highest standards of regional printing. For the writer, the unexpected bonus generated in this work is the friendship of James K. Howard, Northland's young editor of Diné-like patience. Robert Jacobson designed the original edition, and Mary C. Wages the latest one.

For help in later editions, the author extends thanks to editors Stephanie Morrison, Susan McDonald, and Betti Arnold Albrecht of Northland Publishing; to Dan Garland of Garland's Rugs, Sedona; and to Lois and Jerry Jacka of Phoenix for advice and up-to-date images.

Index

Page numbers in *italics* refer to photographs.

A FORMER EDITOR of *Arizona Highways*, Phoenix freelance writer Don Dedera has twenty books and more than fifteen hundred published articles to his credit. In researching this book he went to the sources—weavers, traders, collectors, appraisers, and museum curators—to present a solid introduction to the history and current status of Navajo weaving. Dedera is a graduate of Arizona State University, a recipient of the coveted ASU Achievement Award, the national Ernie Pyle Memorial Award, and the Literary Medal from the National Society of Arts and Letters. He was the first graduate inducted into the Hall of Fame, Walter Cronkite School of Journalism, College of Public Programs at ASU.

Other fine Native American arts and crafts books from Northland Publishing

Beyond Tradition: Contemporary Indian Art and Its Evolution
by Lois Essary Jacka, photographs by Jerry Jacka
with an introduction by Clara Lee Tanner
216 pages, 203 color photographs, includes more than 135 artists,
hardcover and softcover

Clowns of the Hopi: Tradition Keepers and Delight Makers
by Barton Wright, photographs by Jerry Jacka
148 pages, 30 color photographs, 100 color illustrations, softcover

Enduring Traditions: Art of the Navajo
by Lois Essary Jacka, photographs by Jerry Jacka
200 pages, 205 color photographs, includes 194 artists, hardcover

Hopi Kachinas: The Complete Guide to Collecting Kachina Dolls
by Barton Wright
152 pages, 30 color photographs showing 150 kachinas, softcover

Hopi Silver: The History and Hallmarks of Hopi Silversmithing
by Margaret Wright
140 pages, 51 black-and-white photographs, illustrated chart of
hallmarks, softcover

Navajo Jewelry: A Legacy of Silver and Stone
by Lois Essary Jacka, photographs by Jerry Jacka
144 pages, 100 color photographs, softcover

The People Speak: Navajo Folk Art
by Chuck and Jan Rosenak
176 pages, 90 color photographs, includes 41 artists, hardcover

*Trading Post Guidebook: Where to Find the Trading Posts, Galleries,
Auctions, Artists, and Museums of the Four Corners Region*
by Patrick Eddington and Susan Makov
264 pages, 115 color photographs, softcover